FOUL DEEDS & SUSPICIOUS DEATHS IN MANCHESTER

FOUL DEEDS AND SUSPICIOUS DEATHS Series

Foul Deeds and Suspicious Deaths series explores in detail crimes of passion, brutal murders, grisly deeds and foul misdemeanours. From Victorian street crime, to more modern murder where passion, jealousy, or social deprivation brought unexpected violence to those involved. From mysterious death to murder and manslaughter, the books are a fascinating insight into not only those whose lives are forever captured by the suffering they endured, but also into the society that moulded and shaped their lives. Each book takes you on a journey into the darker and unknown side of the area.

Other titles in the series

Foul Deeds and Suspicious Deaths in Blackburn & Hyndburn, Steve Greenhalgh
ISBN: 1-903425-18-2
160pp. Illustrated. £9.99

Foul Deeds and Suspicious Deaths in and around Chesterfield, Geoffrey Sadler
ISBN: 1-903425-30-1
160pp. Illustrated. £9.99

Foul Deeds and Suspicious Deaths in & around Durham, Maureen Anderson
ISBN: 1-903425-46-8
176pp. Illustrated. £9.99

Foul Deeds and Suspicious Deaths in and around Halifax, Stephen Wade
ISBN: 1-903425-45-X
176pp. Illustrated. £9.99

Foul Deeds and Suspicious Deaths in Leeds, David Goodman
ISBN: 1-903425-08-5
176pp. Illustrated. £9.99

Foul Deeds and Suspicious Deaths in Newcastle, Maureen Anderson
ISBN: 1-903425-34-4
176pp. Illustrated. £ 9.99

Foul Deeds and Suspicious Deaths in Nottingham, Kevin Turton
ISBN: 1-903425-35-2
176pp. Illustrated. £9.99

Foul Deeds and Suspicious Deaths around Pontefract and Castleford, Keith Henson
ISBN: 1-903425-54-9
176pp. Illustrated. £ 9.99

Foul Deeds and Suspicious Deaths in and around Rotherham, Kevin Turton
ISBN: 1-903425-27-1
160pp. Illustrated. £9.99

Foul Deeds and Suspicious Deaths Around the Tees, Maureen Anderson
ISBN: 1-903425-26-3
176pp. Illustrated. £9.99

More Foul Deeds and Suspicious Deaths in Wakefield, Kate Taylor
ISBN: 1-903425-48-4
176pp. Illustrated £9.99

Foul Deeds and Suspicious Deaths in York, Keith Henson
ISBN: 1-903425-33-6
176pp. Illustrated. £9.99

Foul Deeds and Suspicious Deaths on the Yorkshire Coast, Alan Whitworth
ISBN: 1-903425-01-8
192pp. Illustrated. £9.99

Please contact us via any of the methods below for more information or a catalogue.
WHARNCLIFFE BOOKS
47 Church Street – Barnsley – South Yorkshire – S70 2AS
Tel: 01226 734555 – 734222 Fax: 01226 734438
E-mail: enquiries@pen-and-sword.co.uk – Website: www.wharncliffebooks.co.uk

Foul Deeds & Suspicious Deaths in

MANCHESTER

MARTIN BAGGOLEY

Series Editor
Brian Elliott

Wharncliffe Books

For Claire

First Published in Great Britain in 2004 by
Wharncliffe Books
an imprint of
Pen and Sword Books Ltd.
47 Church Street
Barnsley
South Yorkshire
S70 2AS

Copyright © Martin Baggoley, 2004

ISBN: 1-903425-65-4

Typeset in 11/13pt Plantin by Mac Style Ltd, Scarborough.

Printed and bound in England by
CPI UK.

Pen and Sword Books Ltd incorporates the Imprints of
Pen & Sword Aviation, Pen & Sword Maritime,
Pen & Sword Military, Wharncliffe Books,
Pen & Sword Select, Pen and Sword Military Classica
and Leo Cooper.

For a complete list of Pen & Sword titles please contact
PEN & SWORD BOOKS LIMITED
47 Church Street
Barnsley
South Yorkshire
S70 2BR
England
E-mail: enquiries@pen-and-sword.co.uk
Website: www.pen-and-sword.co.uk

Contents

William Calcraft, one of the most celebrated hangmen of the nineteenth century, attends to a struggling hooded prisoner at a public execition. Brian Elliott Collection

Introduction and Acknowledgements

ictorian Manchester provides the backdrop to these twelve fascinating and true accounts of murder, manslaughter and mysterious death.

At the time, Manchester was one of the world's major cities that had expanded at an incredible rate during the industrial revolution, with which it will be forever linked. It grew into an important manufacturing and commercial centre, creating great wealth for its leading entrepreneurs. However, there was also an underclass, living in the city's notorious slum districts.

The cases described in this book occurred in locations ranging from its back streets, squalid houses, a prison, workhouse and an exclusive gentlemen's club.

Jealousy, greed and revenge are amongst the motives that lay behind these crimes. The bullet, poison, knives and axes are amongst the methods used by the perpetrators. Their victims included brutalized wives, a prison officer, a police sergeant and a workhouse inmate.

Each crime is of course unique, and involves a great deal of human tragedy. There are the victims, of course, and their friends and families, who continued to suffer emotionally for the remainder of their lives. Whilst some may have difficulty to feel anything other than disgust and revulsion at the actions of the killers, it should be remembered that they too had friends and families who cared for them, and who suffered emotional pain due to their actions. Some of the most poignant moments in the book, are the goodbyes said by the distraught parents, wives and children of the condemned.

This was a significant period in the development of the criminal justice system. Prior to 1868 executions took place in public, outside of prison walls, and that was the fate that awaited the condemned in the early chapters of the book. The officers of the Manchester police force, both uniformed and the detectives, were determined, brave and in the absence of forensic science to support them, surprisingly successful.

Manchester was, and remains a wonderful city, but as in the case of any other place, it has its darker side, which these cases illuminate.

I wish to thank S C Hunter and Geoff Parker for their help with the illustrations. I am grateful to the editor of the *Manchester Evening News,* an invaluable source of information for anyone interested in the history of any aspect of Manchester and its people. Thanks also to my daughter Rachel for her typing skills.

CHAPTER 1

The Manchester Poisoning Case 1856

ohn Monaghan, a whisky drinking sixty-year-old varnish maker, died at 11 Hope Street, Chorlton, the home of his daughter Eliza and her husband Francis Keene, with whom he had lived, on 11 August 1855. Dr J Hatton was called, who gave the cause of death as chronic dysentery, and John was later buried at St Wilfrid's Roman Catholic Church in Hulme.

Francis had taken out an insurance policy in the sum of £10 16s (£10 80p) on his father-in-law's life, and as there seemed to be no suspicious circumstances, the Wellington Insurance Company paid out. It is probable that the death would have passed unnoticed had not John's son James taken

St Wilfrid's Church remains very much as it was in the 1850s, when John Monaghan was buried there. A few months after his burial, it was to become the setting for a macabre exhumation. The author

out a policy with the Diadem Life Assurance Company, for the then huge sum of £300. When James claimed the money, the suspicious company refused to pay, so James initiated civil proceedings and the case was listed for February 1856 in the Court of the Exchequer. Diadem's solicitor, Thomas Rogers of Fenchurch Street, London, sent his principal clerk, Charles Bradlaugh, to Manchester to make further enquiries.

On his arrival, Mr Bradlaugh unearthed a good deal of circumstantial evidence pointing to a conspiracy involving several people, to murder John Monaghan, and to claim the insurance money by means of forgery and perjury. Thus, in the early months of 1856 the country was fascinated by what became known as the 'Manchester Poisoning Case,' which developed into a classic Victorian court room drama, played out in the city's police and coroner's courts, and eventually at the Liverpool Assizes.

Mr Bradlaugh discovered that Diadem's Manchester agent, twenty-two-year-old Edward Dunn, who had agreed to the policy, which gave John's age as being ten years younger than he actually was, had been responsible for several thefts. This included the misappropriation of a cheque for £15 4s 9d (£15 24p) which should have been paid to the widow of a policy holder. Satisfied that he had participated in the conspiracy, Mr Bradlaugh had him arrested on these other charges, and he was committed to the Assizes in custody, facing the possibility of penal transportation.

Mr Bradlaugh also discovered incriminating circumstantial evidence against other individuals and asked Superintendent Leary of the city's 'C' Division, to arrest James Monaghan, a stay maker and son of the deceased, George Barry a stall holder in the local Smithfield Market, along with Thomas Bull Holland, a surgeon. All appeared before the city's police court on 23 January 1856. Mr Bradlaugh acted as prosecutor and advised the court that he would offer no evidence against Dr Holland who was released from the dock. However, he was to be called as a prosecution witness, as it was suggested that the others had used the doctor to gain knowledge of poisons, and in particular acetate of lead. In offering no evidence against him, he was acknowledging that this had been done unwittingly by Dr Holland.

As yet, there had been no post-mortem on John Monaghan's body, but this was in hand, and Mr Bradlaugh advised the magistrates that he would be asking for the defendants to be kept in custody, as he intended to demonstrate that they had the motive, means and opportunity of committing the murder. The motive was the £300 insurance policy, the means was by administering acetate of lead, and as for the opportunity, he contended that James had poisoned his father's whiskies over a period of time.

Thomas Bull Holland was a rather sad figure in the witness box. Until two years earlier he had been in a successful practice with another surgeon, Edward Watson, but this ended, due mainly to Dr Holland's increasing dependence on alcohol. He faced several hours of questioning by Mr Bradlaugh, and his evidence was marked by much hesitancy and claims of being unable to remember many events.

Mr Bradlaugh knew of several meetings that the doctor had had with the accused, and he attempted to demonstrate that they had sought information about poisons from him. The dates of these meetings were crucial to the prosecution, as Mr Bradlaugh suggested that they took place before John's death. Under questioning, Dr Holland admitted knowing Dunn before the death but insisted that he had not met James Monaghan until September 1855, after the death. This followed a visit the doctor had made to his home, which had been arranged by Dunn, regarding an insurance policy in respect of a sister of James, named Sarah. Furthermore, Dr Holland insisted that he had not met Barry until October 1855, again following the death of John Monaghan.

Dr Holland admitted to a number of meetings with the accused over a period of several weeks, and many of these took place in local public houses such as the *Rolla Inn*, on Collier Street, Salford, and the *Oxford Tavern* on Oxford Road, Manchester. He confirmed that on one occasion when all three of the accused were present they had discussed the insurance policy and wondered whether it would be paid, so that they could go to Australia as planned. The men had also visited him at his home on several occasions and he recalled being asked by Dunn about acetate of lead. The doctor had advised him that it could be used in small doses as medicine in the treatment of dysentery, but if used in larger doses it acted as a poison. Dunn had been interested in the fact that when acetate of lead was added to water the liquid turned milky, but when added to whisky, there was no effect on the appearance of the spirit in the glass.

Dr Holland acknowledged that these meetings did take place and the matters raised by Mr Bradlaugh had been discussed, but they had occurred after John's death and could not therefore have been part of a conspiracy to murder him. He advised the court that he was able to state this categorically as they took place at about the time of the Manchester autumn race meeting in September 1855. Mr Bradlaugh advised the court that he would produce evidence to show that the witness was confused and that they had in fact occurred at the time of the other race meeting, namely that held in May 1855, that is before John's death.

Mr Fearnley represented all of the defendants except for Barry, who was represented by Mr E S Bent. Both solicitors argued that there was insufficient evidence to hold their clients and the case against them should be dismissed. The magistrates retired for fifteen minutes and upon returning stated that in their view there were suspicious circumstances surrounding the death of John Monaghan, which required further investigation. The prisoners were remanded in custody for a week, but the magistrates agreed that a bail application could be made on the following day. Mr Bradlaugh asked that Dr Holland should be remanded in custody also, but not surprisingly this rather strange request was dismissed summarily by the magistrates.

At the following day's bail hearing, the defence argued that the prosecution case was based purely on circumstantial evidence, and it had not been shown that John Monaghan had been poisoned, let alone which poison had been used. Furthermore, the accused had not been arrested following a coroner's jury verdict, but simply at the request of a biased individual, out to protect the interests of the Diadem Company.

Mr Bradlaugh responded by confirming that he had applied to Mr Herford the city coroner, to exhume John Monaghan's body, and work was due to start later that day. After just a few minutes deliberation, the magistrates refused bail.

Mr E Herford gave his permission and the exhumation began on 24 January, five labourers having been hired for the task. Some relatives of the deceased indicated where the coffin had supposedly been buried and this was confirmed by Mr Timperley, the undertaker. He also suggested that the coffin would be easily identifiable as there was a distinctive zinc plate inscribed with the deceased's name and date of internment, which he had made and fastened to the coffin lid. However, the coffin was not where it was said to have been, and the subsequent search for John Monaghan's body became perhaps the most macabre feature of any murder investigation in Manchester's history. The labourers continued to dig until midnight, by which time the body had still not been located. The search resumed the following morning, but despite digging until 6 pm, John Monaghan's body could still not be found.

The third day's search was also unsuccessful, and by now a number of rumours had begun to circulate throughout Manchester. One suggested that the accused had removed the coffin and body before the investigation began. It was the custom at St Wilfrid's to place three coffins in one hole, and until the third was put in, only a temporary covering was used, which made the removal of one relatively easy. A wall surrounded the graveyard but there was a large hole in it, making it easy to remove a coffin from the site. Another rumour suggested that they had simply removed the zinc plate, thus making identification of the coffin more difficult.

Work stopped at 11 pm on the third night and by then, forty-seven graves had been opened, and the coffin lids raised to allow Mr Timperley, who had known the deceased, to identify him. The disturbance of so many bodies, in various stages of decomposition, had led to a highly offensive smell to permeate the surrounding neighbourhood, which led to many complaints. Furthermore, some relatives of those buried in the graveyard expressed their concern and distress at the exhumations.

However, Mr Bradlaugh was not to be deterred by such considerations. If the fourth day's labours proved unsuccessful, he had arranged for more labourers to be hired to open up all of the remaining graves if necessary, to either locate the body or confirm it was not in the graveyard. Fortunately, this was not to be necessary as at 3.30 pm that day, the coffin, complete with zinc plate, was located, and Mr Timperley identified the body. This was much to the relief of all concerned, including the five labourers, each of whom earned a bonus of two sovereigns.

As the accused languished in their cells awaiting their next appearance at the police court, the inquest on John Monaghan opened on 29 January, before Mr Herford, the city coroner, at his office in Ridgefield. A jury had been formed and they all made their way to view the body, as was the custom at the time, in the porch of St Wilfrid's. Upon their arrival, the lid was raised and, fortunately, a large amount of disinfectant had been applied to take away the worst of the smell.

In the months since John's death there had been some decomposition, and his eyes had gone, but his features were recognisable. Mr Timperley formally identified him together with the zinc plate, and Mrs Timperley identified the shroud in which he had been buried, and which she had made.

Mr Herford adjourned the inquest until 6 February, and in the interim he arranged for a surgeon, Mr T W Dyson, to

The porch of St Wilfrid's Church, in which John Monaghan's body was displayed for the coroner's jury. The author

perform a surgical post-mortem assisted by Dr Hatton. It was agreed that a doctor appointed by the defence could be present. The viscera were to be removed and sent for separate chemical analysis.

On 30 January, the prisoners appeared at the police court and Mr Bradlaugh advised the magistrates that the results of the post-mortem were still awaited, but he advised the court that he had important evidence to present regarding the timing of the meetings the accused had with Dr Holland. To establish that they occurred before the death and not after, as Dr Holland had insisted, he called Matthew Hall, landlord of the *Rolla Inn* who confirmed that he knew Dr Holland and James Monaghan, who had met several times in his establishment. These had taken place in May 1855, several months before the death of John Monaghan. He was certain that they occurred at the time of the May meeting at Manchester Racecourse, as he recalled getting ready to go to the course and on one occasion they were present, and as he did not attend the Autumn meeting, it must have been in May.

The prosecutor then called his surprise witness, William Monaghan, a London policeman, and brother of the accused. William testified that he had visited Manchester three weeks before his father's death, and James had told him of the policy with Diadem. William had replied by suggesting that given their father's age it would undoubtedly cost a large amount of money. James told him that his correct age had not been given. William reminded his brother that if this was discovered he faced penal transportation. William continued his damaging testimony by stating that James had also produced a proposal for a policy on his father's life with the Tradesman's Mutual Insurance Company for £1,000, which was not in their father's handwriting. Upon hearing of his father's death, William had become suspicious and had agreed to attend court as a witness to 'further the ends of justice, and if necessary find evidence which incriminated James.'

Having heard this testimony the magistrates again stated that there was evidence suggesting that the death of John Monaghan had been suspicious, and they remanded the accused in custody, to reappear after the results of the post-mortem were known, and the conclusion of the inquest.

The first to give evidence at the inquest, held on 6 February was Professor Frankland of the chemistry department at Owens College. He advised the court that the police had sent him five sealed jars, which contained the deceased's viscera. One contained the stomach and intestines; the second his liver; the third his bladder; the fourth his brain and the fifth his lungs.

The professor continued his evidence by stating that he had tested all of these for evidence of the presence of a number of poisons, such as lead, arsenic, antimony and mercury. In the stomach he had found a trace of zinc; in the liver a trace of lead and copper; in the kidneys a trace of zinc; and in the lungs and brains there was no trace of any substances. He concluded by stating categorically there was no evidence whatsoever of death by poisoning.

When asked by Mr Herford if he was certain of his findings, especially in so far as lead was concerned, the professor was adamant. The quantity of lead that he found was comparable to that which would be found in an individual who drank

Owens College in the 1850s, by which time it was already the centre of scientific learning in Manchester. Under the guidance of scientists such as Professor Frankland, it was to play a significant role in the development of forensic pathology in the city. J E Cornish

THE OLD OWENS COLLEGE

water provided through a lead pipe. If the deceased had been poisoned by lead, he would have found it in much larger quantities, even allowing for decomposition of the body. He also confirmed that acetate of lead was given medicinally in cases of dysentery and diarrhoea, and if the deceased had been taking it for such a reason, that would account for the amount found in his body. There was no challenge by Mr Bradlaugh.

The next witness was the surgeon, Dr Dyson, who stated that he and his colleague, Dr Hatton, had performed a post-mortem at the Chorlton Union Workhouse, where the body had been taken from the graveyard following its exhumation. He described the body as being extremely emaciated, the abdomen being depressed as far as the spine. The eyes had gone, and the nose and cheeks had been reduced to a pulpy mass. The lower extremities were much decayed, especially the left thigh. Dr Dyson also confirmed that he had seen the viscera. Dr Dyson stated that he had found no evidence of the existence of acetate of lead in quantities sufficient to poison the deceased.

Mr Bradlaugh, however, was not beaten yet, and he challenged Dr Dyson by suggesting that medical opinion was divided on the question of the absorption of acetate of lead. To reinforce this point he produced a copy of *Taylor's Medical Jurispudence,* and began reading from it 'It has been a question.....' Before he could get any further, a rather smug Mr Fearnley, solicitor for the defence, rose to his feet. He advised the court that he had the latest edition of *Taylor's Medical Jurispudence,* and noted that the relevant sentence had been amended to read 'it was **formerly** a question....'

A disconsolate Mr Bradlaugh sat silently as the next witness, John Hatton, Doctor to the Chorlton Workhouse explained that he had treated John Monaghan, who had been suffering from a serious case of dysentery and diarrhoea. On 26 July 1855 he had prescribed sulphate copper, on 30 July he had prescribed a medicine containing zinc, and on 2 August a mixture containing acetate of lead. Four bottles of this last mentioned mixture had been taken by the deceased, and this meant he had consumed a total of sixty-four grains of acetate of lead.

Dr Hatton concluded that death was simply due to the fact that 'he was an old man, breaking up in his constitution, and the soft mucous membrane of the bowels, found during the post-mortem, caused diarrhoea and dysentery,' and whilst treating him he had seen no signs of poisoning.

The coroner's jury found that John Monaghan's death was not a result of being poisoned, and he had not been murdered. Mr Bradlaugh's case was in tatters, and he had no alternative other than to withdraw the charges of murder against James Monaghan, Dunn and Barry. 'The Manchester Poisoning Case' had come to an end, or almost.

Mr Bradlaugh faced considerable criticism in the press and the *Manchester Guardian* was particularly scathing. It published an editorial criticising the prosecution of the murder case, as it had relied solely on circumstantial evidence, rumour and hearsay. It was especially critical of the mass exhumation.

This drew a response from an indignant Mr Bradlaugh, who reminded the editor that several men still faced serious charges relating to forgery and perjury.

The final act of the drama was played out at Liverpool Assizes before His Lordship Baron Martin, in late March 1856. Before him were James Monaghan, Terence McLoughlin and Edward Dunn, all of whom were charged with forging the will, and James Keefe, who was charged with being an accessory after the fact. Dunn was also tried for the unrelated matters stemming from his employment as agent for Diadem. During this trial, many answers were provided regarding the will. It was acknowledged by all of the parties that the deceased had not known of the £300 policy on his life, and it had been established that James Monaghan and Dunn had taken the policy out and paid the premiums themselves up to John's death.

A few days before John's death, his son-in-law, Francis Keene, had made out a will stating that the policy for £10 16 shillings (£10 80p), which he had taken out with the Wellington Insurance Company, was left to his wife, Eliza. After John's death, Francis attempted to prove the will, but was unsuccessful as certain legal formalities had not been completed, thus making that document worthless. Francis took it home and forgot about it.

However, some time later, James Monaghan and Dunn visited Keene's home, and the latter noticed Dunn reading the will and later making additions with a pencil. After he had finished he said 'It's as good a will as if I'd paid a lawyer to draw it up.' On 13 September 1855 James Monaghan asked an acquaintance, Michael O'Neill, to write out a document which James dictated to him, and which purported to be his father's will. However, when asked to sign it with what was supposed to be John's mark, O'Neill refused, but Terence McLaughlin was later persuaded to put the mark on the document.

When James attempted to process the will it was deemed unacceptable as it had not in fact been properly drawn up and witnessed. James took the document away and later returned with James Keefe, who swore that he was a witness to the will and had seen John make his mark.

Following the intervention of Mr Bradlaugh, the police later searched James Monaghan's home and in a trunk they found the document which Francis Keene confirmed was the original will he had written out, and upon which were the alterations made in pencil by Dunn.

The defence argued that the charges stemmed from Diadem not wishing to pay the £300 on the policy, which was rightfully James Monaghan's. In his summing up the judge suggested that this was an important case as it raised significant issues relating to the insuring of lives on individuals without their knowledge, which to some extent vindicated Mr Bradlaugh. The judge discussed the background to the case, including the original murder charges, but suggested that from the evidence he had heard James had been a loving and caring son, who had been devoted to his father. Nevertheless, the summing up left nobody in any doubt that he considered there to have been an act of forgery committed in this case.

The jury found all of the defendants except for James not guilty on all charges. James was found guilty of forgery and was sentenced to six months imprisonment.

The curtain had finally closed on 'The Manchester Poisoning Case,' which demonstrated the limitations of circumstantial evidence, no matter how incriminating it might seem, and no matter how suspicious the death appeared to be. The case also highlighted the significance forensic pathology was to play in future murder investigations.

CHAPTER 2

Revenge in South King Street
1862

van Meller, a fifty-eight-year-old house agent, had his business premises on the second floor of St James's Chambers, South King Street, in the centre of Manchester. His eldest son, John, was his junior partner, and his youngest boy, William, was employed as an assistant clerk.

At 8.45 am on Friday, 16 May 1862, William was the first to arrive for work, and he knew that his father would be arriving soon. However, the next to arrive was a tenant of one of their properties at 5 Britannia Buildings, Ducie Street, in the Strangeways district. His name was William Robert Taylor who was thirty-seven-year-old, who was accompanied by his twenty-three-year-old wife, Martha Ann.

Mr Taylor had been a regular visitor at the office since first renting the property on 1 October 1861, as since then a series of incidents had soured the relationship between Evan Meller and his tenant. However, young Meller had no hesitation in inviting the Taylors to sit in the ante-room to await his father's arrival, whilst he returned into his own room to begin work.

St James's Chambers. Manchester Central Library Local Studies and Archives

View of the Outside of Mr. Meller's Office, St. James's Chambers, South King Street.

At a few minutes after nine o'clock, the young man heard his father enter the office and greet the Taylors. However, almost immediately after the greeting he heard his father desperately cry out 'Oh! Mr Taylor.' His son ran towards the door leading into the ante-room, to be met, he later claimed, by Mrs Taylor holding a revolver in her extended arms, aimed at his face, which forced him to retreat back into his room.

At about the same time, Joseph Leatherbrow, a spirit merchant with an office directly below those of the Mellers, heard the sound of what he thought was that of someone falling down the staircase. He went out on to the landing to find Mr Meller lying unconscious at the foot of the stairs.

Mr Leatherbrow knelt down at the side of the obviously dying man, and called to John Hooley, his cellarman, to bring a glass of water. Mr Hooley did so, and as the two men held the dying man's head up, they saw William Taylor walking calmly down the stairs towards them, holding a revolver in his hand. They watched incredulously, as he put the revolver at Evan Meller's head and fired. He missed his target, but the ball passed through the right arm of John Hooley, before entering his knee.

The cellarman managed to lift himself up and he made his way downstairs, followed by his assailant. However, when they both reached the ground floor, Taylor did not attempt to shoot him again, but apologised, and advised him to seek medical assistance as soon as possible at the Manchester Royal Infirmary.

William Meller, meanwhile, had heard the shot and ran downstairs to where his father now lay. Before doing so, he had raised the alarm by shouting into the street below, and his cries for help had been heard by Henry Pankhurst, an auctioneer, who was walking along South King Street at the time. He entered St James's Chambers, where he saw the wounded Hooley, writhing in agony, and he noticed Martha Taylor standing nearby.

Pankhurst climbed the stairs on to the first floor landing, to be met by the sight of the mortally wounded victim lying on his back. He took hold of his wrist and felt a weak pulse, and he also noticed that there were several cuts in his clothing, and

The Scene of the Murder of Mr. Meller.

Courtesy of Manchester Central Library (Local Studies and Archives)

that he was saturated in blood, suggesting he had been the victim of a knife attack. He again felt for a pulse, but now there was no sign of life.

William Meller was close to his father, and put his own face next to that of the older man, to kiss him. As he did so, Taylor raised his arm and pointed the revolver at the youngster, as though preparing to shoot. Pankhurst bravely put his hand out towards the revolver, and exclaimed 'Good God, man, what are you going to do?' Taylor dropped his arm and revolver to his side and cried 'He has ruined me and my family.'

The police had been alerted and Pankhurst remained standing close to Taylor, ensuring he did not escape, as they awaited their arrival. Pankhurst warned the officers that Taylor still had the gun, but he was easily disarmed. Pankhurst, who had acted throughout the incident with great calmness and bravery, and had probably saved the life of William Meller, was not finished yet. He returned to the first floor landing to assist in carrying Mr Meller's body down to the street, which he then accompanied to the Royal Infirmary.

The police officers who had attended the incident were Sergeants Thomas Bramall and Henry Bateman. Having seized the revolver, and detained Taylor, they ensured that the dead and wounded victims had been taken by cab to the Infirmary. They then searched the building, and in the deceased's office, they found what turned out to be the murder weapon; this was a foot long cheese knife, which was one and a half inches wide, and which was stained with blood.

It was stained right up to the handle, which indicated that the entire blade had been thrust into the victim's body. Traces of blood were found along the entire second flight of stairs in St James's Chambers, which confirmed that the attack had started on the second floor, and as the deceased stepped backwards, it had continued as he tumbled downwards to the first floor landing, where there was a large pool of blood. There was little doubt that the victim had been subjected to a sustained and vicious attack.

After being charged with the murder of Meller, Taylor exclaimed 'Thank God I have finished my work.' Sergeant Bateman searched him and found a powder flask, percussion caps and a sheath, into which the cheese knife fitted snugly. It was at this stage that Mrs Taylor arrived at the police office, asking about her husband. She had approached an officer at the scene, but in the confusion, she had not been detained, but she was now.

News about this sensational crime had spread rapidly about the city, and by the late morning, Thomas Jones, of Messrs Jones and Melrose, of Deansgate, arrived at the police office. He confirmed that on the previous Tuesday afternoon, the prisoner came to his shop to buy a revolver. After inspecting several weapons, he chose a six barrelled revolver, the price of which was one sovereign. However, Taylor had no money, but he offered a silver Geneva watch in exchange. Mr Jones agreed even though the watch was not working properly, and the shopkeeper included a bullet mould in the transaction. Mr Jones was able to identify the weapon, and also Taylor as the purchaser.

The police had also managed to find Martha Woolley who cleaned the Meller premises every day. She had cleaned them that morning at 8 am, before the crimes were committed, and she was able to confirm that the cheese knife had not been there then. By late morning, the police had located both of the weapons used in the crimes.

Sergeant Bateman had also found three keys on Taylor, who advised the officer that they belonged to 5 Britannia Buildings. He also told the sergeant that he would find something of interest at the house, but he would not elaborate. Bateman took a colleague, Sergeant Watson, to the house, and even though both were experienced police officers, they were not prepared for the horrible scene with which they were confronted in one of the bedrooms.

They unlocked the door to a dark and miserable room, and there, lay on old newspapers on the floor, were the bodies of three children, who from the state of decomposition, had been there for several days. Both of the sergeants became distressed, but having regained their composure, they summoned Doctors Winterbottom and Clayton, whose practice was close by; however, it was obvious that the children were beyond medical assistance.

The children had been carefully washed and laid out as though in a funeral parlour. They were dressed in clean clothing, and around each of their necks and waists, were tied pieces of black ribbon. Each was wearing a clean pair of stockings, and the winding-sheet of each child was one of their father's shirts, for these were indeed the children of William Taylor.

A piece of paper had been pinned to the chest of each of the bodies, which contained a similar note, which read:

> *We are six, one at Harpurhey lies, and thither our bodies take. Meller and son are our cruel murderers, but God and our loving parents will avenge us. Love rules here: we are all gone to our sister, to part no more.*

On the reverse side of each of the pieces of paper was the name and age of the individual children, and they read as follows:

> *Mary Hannah Taylor, 12 years of age.*
> *Hannah Mariah Taylor, 8 years of age.*
> *William Robert Taylor, 5 years of age.*

Also on the centre body, which was that of the youngest girl, was another piece of paper, which contained the following message:

> *Meller our sister slew through gross neglect.*

The references to Meller being the cause of a sister's death, pointed to the

VIEW of the MURDERERS' H(
in Britannia Buildings, Ducie S
Strangeways.

Courtesy of Manchester Central Library (Local Studies and Archives)

motive that lay behind the murder of the agent by his tenant. That was the death of Taylor's daughter, which had occurred several months earlier, and for which the grieving father blamed Meller. These and other details would emerge in the days that followed, and eventually at the trial itself. For now it was essential to establish the causes of death, and the coroner wasted no time in summoning a jury, for the inquest opened at just after noon 16 May, only three hours after Meller had been murdered.

William Heath, house surgeon at the Royal Infirmary, arrived later that afternoon, having just completed the post-mortem on Meller. He was dead on arrival, and on examining the body, eleven stab wounds were found, and they covered the whole of the body, indicating a frenzied attack. There were two wounds to the chest, which had been the cause of death: one to the right, was just under twelve inches deep, and had penetrated the breast bone and left ventricle of the heart, and it had then passed through the diaphragm, and into the liver; the wound to the left passed through the sixth and seventh ribs, and again penetrated the left ventricle of the heart. There were other serious stab wounds, amongst which was a wound through his back, which had reached a lung, and there were two wounds to the left buttock. There were also deep cuts to the left forearm and to his hands, sustained as the victim attempted to defend himself. Dr Heath agreed that the cheese knife could have caused the injuries.

However, the question of how the children had died would prove to be more problematic. In the early afternoon, the eighteen members of the jury visited the Taylor home to view the bodies of the children, and as they entered the bedroom where they lay, they came across Dr Winterbottom performing a post-mortem on Mary Hannah Taylor, which must have been a chilling sight. At the inquest, later that day, Dr Winterbottom shared his findings.

The doctor had found every one of the young girl's organs to have been healthy and normal. On opening the stomach there had been a few ounces of fluid, which he thought was barley water, and there was no odour indicating the presence of a poison. There were no marks which would suggest strangulation and there was no evidence of any violence. When asked by the coroner Mr Herford for a cause of death, the doctor could not be specific, but thought that some as yet undetected poison had probably been used. She had been dead for about two days, and he was certain that she had not died due to natural causes. The hearing was adjourned until the following Monday, so that Mary Hannah's stomach could be analysed, which the coroner insisted should be completed by Monday morning.

The investigations into the young girl's stomach, and the subsequent ones into those of her brother and sister were to be controversial and could have potentially undermined the confidence of the public in the abilities of Manchester's scientists to help solve murder cases when poisons had been used. This may have been avoided had the coroner not insisted on such a quick analysis being made that weekend. The most appropriate person to consult was Professor Daniel Stone, a respected and experienced analyst, of the Royal Manchester School of Medicine. And so it was that on the morning of Saturday, 17 May, a police officer arrived at the school, carrying a jar containing the stomach, and asked for Professor Stone. The officer was informed by the janitor that the professor did not attend the school on Saturday, but he would be at work early on Monday morning. The officer replied that this would be too late and left, which meant that the opportunity of having the analysis done by one of the country's leading authorities in the field was lost. As concern grew over the following days about the apparent lack of progress in discovering the cause of death, the professor felt compelled to clarify what had happened, by writing to the *Manchester Guardian,* and his letter concluded by stating:

> *In all poisoning cases which have been brought before me at this School, I have had ready and crucial assistance from my colleagues, and I am sure that the Strangeways murder would not have formed an exception, as with their aid, I believe many of the difficulties which now surround it might have been obviated.*

The stomach was eventually taken to Fearnside Hudson, Analytical Chemist and Government Science Master, based at his laboratory at 68 Corporation Street, during Saturday afternoon. He later attended a post-mortem being conducted by the surgeon, Mr Robert Heywood McKeand, on the two other children, and was given their stomachs also. Sergeants Bateman and Watson also brought him some pots, bottles, pans, sugar, coffee and sago from the Taylor home for analysis, as it was thought they may possibly contain traces of poisons.

He tested the body parts and other items for all types of poison, including arsenic, mercury, lead, antimony, copper, zinc, prussic and other acids, and laudanum, but he found no trace. When he advised the coroner's court of these findings at the adjourned hearing on Monday, there was an audible expression of astonishment and disbelief by several members of the jury, which the coroner admonished them for.

Dr McKeand described similar results of his post-mortems on the two other children, to those given by Dr Winterbottom, and when pressed by the coroner could offer no cause for their deaths.

The coroner's jury returned after forty-five minutes with their findings, which were that Evan Meller had been murdered by William Robert Taylor, and Martha Ann Taylor had been an accessory. The jury was convinced that the children did not die from natural causes or accidentally, but were murdered by persons unknown.

There was widespread public alarm following the failure to find any cause of death in respect of the children, which was reflected in the local press coverage of the case. Attention focussed on the brief period of time allowed by the coroner for the analysis to be made, and there was implicit criticism of Dr Hudson, his equipment and methods used. The chief constable, Captain Palin, was especially concerned about the possible loss of confidence in the local criminal justice system and the police. At a meeting of the watch committee therefore on Wednesday 21 May, Captain Palin persuaded its members to agree to an analysis of the three children's stomachs being performed by the renowned Professor A Taylor of Guy's Hospital, London. The professor had been telegraphed and had accepted the commission, and Sergeant Bateman was entrusted with the task of taking the stomachs, in their respective jars to London that night by train. Having done so, he was to travel to Somerset to make further enquiries into the Taylors' backgrounds as they had lived there before moving to Manchester.

To his credit, Dr Hudson accepted the position, and in letters to local newspapers, he defended his qualifications, which were many, his equipment and his methods. He was confident that Professor Taylor would simply confirm his own findings.

The coroner had given permission for the funerals of the three children and Mr Meller to go ahead. The children would normally have had to be buried in paupers' graves, had it not been for the intervention of Mr B Lee of 25 Sagar Street, who pinned a notice on the shutters of 5 Britannia Buildings, inviting contributions towards their funeral expenses. There was an overwhelming response, and more than enough cash was collected, mostly in very small amounts, from the district's poorest residents. They were buried in Harpurhey cemetery, as their sister had been some months earlier, on Monday, 19 May. Enough money had been raised to purchase a grave, stone and three coffins made of oak. A large crowd gathered to watch the hearse leave the home, where their bodies had been kept over the weekend, and several carts were used as standing places along the route.

Mr Meller's family had hoped for a quiet and private funeral, on the following day but such was the widespread interest in the case that several hundred spectators lined the route from the family home in Almondbury Place, Cornbrook, to the parish church at Chorlton-cum-Hardy. He was buried alongside his wife, two years to the day since she died.

Professor Taylor received the jars and their gruesome contents on 22 May and immediately began his analysis, which had been completed by the time the committal hearing was held on 30 May. He travelled to Manchester and presented his findings before a packed and hushed magistrates court. To everyone's surprise they were essentially the same as those previously given, as he had found no trace whatsoever of poison in the children, and he was certain that poison had not been administered in liquid or solid form. He had also eliminated hanging, strangulation, drowning, starvation and suffocation as possible causes.

However, he was convinced that they did not die from natural causes, and he put forward one suggestion as to how death may have occurred, but acknowledged he could offer no proof to back up his theory. He stated that they could have been poisoned by chloroform in vapour form, because if used in this manner, all trace would disappear within just a few hours, and as the Taylor children had been dead for a few days, that would explain the absence of any trace of it. Professor Taylor told the court 'a teaspoon full and even less, in vapour, has been known to destroy life in the short period of two minutes: the power of detecting it in the blood and viscera is limited to a very short period after death. The longest I ever traced it is twenty-four hours.'

This inability to conclusively determine just how the children died meant that William and Martha Taylor would later stand trial for the murder of the adult victim only. This was despite Sergeant Bateman locating a former work colleague of William, in Somerset, who could positively identify the handwriting on the pieces of paper on the children's chests as that of their father: this was simply not sufficient proof.

Their trial took place on Saturday 23 August in St George's Hall, Liverpool, before the judge, Mr Baron Wilde. Such had been the continued interest in the case that admission to the court was by ticket only.

The prosecution case was built around those witnesses who had been present at the time that the murder occurred or shortly afterwards, including John Hooley, who had made a full recovery from his wounds. When the defence cross examined the victims' sons, some explanation was presented to the jury as to why the accused felt so bitterly towards the agent.

William Taylor became tenant of 5 Britannia Buildings on 1 October 1861. The premises comprised adequate living space for the family, and at the front there was a shop, which he intended to open as a general provisions store. The quarterly rent of £12 was not payable in advance, but the new tenant paid £10 for the fixtures and fittings. There was a bathroom on the second floor, which was supplied with hot water from a

WILLIAM ROBERT TAYLOR.
Taken at the Court, on Monday.

Courtesy of Manchester Central Library (Local Studies and Archives)

boiler behind the kitchen fire. Shortly after the Taylors moved in, the water pipes began leaking badly, and after they advised Mr Meller, a plumber was sent to repair them. However, a few days later they began leaking again, and despite several requests from Taylor, no further repairs were carried out.

During the evening of Sunday, 19 February 1862, the boiler exploded. All of the family were at home, but their daughter, Harriet Jane, was sat in front of the fire, and took the full force of the explosion. She was blown across the room, and was badly scalded and wounded by hot coals, heavy pieces of iron, and by the stones from either side of the fireplace, which were blown out. Suffering terrible injuries to her entire body, she died twenty hours later. One of her feet had been blown off, and although probably totally destroyed in the explosion, her distraught father spent the days leading up to her funeral in a desperate but unsuccessful search for it amongst the debris.

The inquest on Harriet found that she had suffered an accidental death, but the jury did criticise the Mellers. No doubt the Taylors thought that this verdict would help in their claim for £500 compensation from the agent, but they were proved wrong, for Mr Meller told his tenant that the explosion had been his own fault as he had allowed the pipes to freeze in the cold weather, and no compensation would be paid. This added to William Taylor's sense of outrage and injustice, which he already felt, after bailiffs were sent into the premises, when he refused to pay the rent due at Christmas. Most of the family's possession were seized and auctioned in lieu of payment. By now the shop was no longer open, and the family was living in poverty.

In February 1862, Taylor found a new tenant for the premises, Mr Godden, who was prepared to take over the lease. A meeting with Mr Meller was arranged, at which the agent heard that Mr Godden had agreed to pay Taylor £35 for the fixtures and fittings: Mr Meller felt obliged to tell him that they were not Taylor's property and he could not sell them, whereupon Mr Godden cancelled the arrangement. This infuriated Taylor even more, and intensified his antagonism towards Meller.

When the rent fell due again on 25 March, Taylor would not, or more likely could not pay. At this point it probably needs to be emphasised that Evan Meller was a highly respected businessman, who had acted for prestigious clients which included Manchester Grammar School. Throughout his transactions with Taylor, the agent was acting in the best interests of the owner of 5 Britannia Buildings whom he represented. It was at this point that the agent offered Taylor a way out, which was that he need not pay the rent and no action would be taken against him if he and his family simply moved out and vacated the premises. However, the offer was refused and the bailiffs again forced their way in and took what little was left, and this occurred on 30 April, just two weeks before Taylor took his revenge.

The jury at the trial was thus aware of this background to the case, and the defence called no witnesses, but argued that Taylor was insane at the time of the crime. The killing of Evan Meller was portrayed not as a premeditated act of revenge, but the desperate act of a man behaving under the delusion that the victim was the cause of all his problems, including the deaths of his four children.

As for Martha, it was suggested to the jury that she had not known of her husband's plans, when they visited St James's Chambers on the fateful morning. Credence could not be given to this version of events if an explanation could not be found for William Meller's claim that she had pointed a revolver at his face. The defence acknowledged that he would not lie about such a thing but they simply argued that he was wrong and had made a mistake in all of the excitement. Her behaviour after the crime, which included making a false confession at one stage, was portrayed as evidence of a wife standing by a beloved husband, and that a distinction needed to be made between that and her acting as an accessory to murder.

The jury retired at 2.23 pm and returned twenty-two minutes later, having found William guilty, and Martha not guilty. She was immediately removed from the dock and sentence of death was passed on her husband. There was no recommendation for mercy, and the judge advised him that

MARY ANN TAYLOR.
Taken at the Court, on M onday.

The publishers of the broadsheet, from which the portrait is taken, got Marta's name wrong. Manchester Central Library (Local Studies and Archives)

there was no hope of a reprieve and that he had only a relatively few days of life remaining to him.

Before being taken from the court to Kirkdale gaol, he was allowed a final meeting with his seventy-year-old father, his sister and his niece. His sister asked him how the children had died but he refused to discuss the subject. They returned to their native Somerset, but not before visiting the graves of the children. They also called on Mr Lee to thank him for his kindness in arranging for the funerals: almost immediately, a rumour spread throughout the neighbourhood that the murderer's wife was there and the house was quickly besieged by a large crowd, which had to be dispersed by the police.

The Taylors had remained close throughout the proceedings, and she decided to take lodgings in Liverpool, where she intended staying until after the execution. However, her father had also travelled from Somerset, and persuaded her to return there with him. She did so on Friday, 29 August, and when she told her husband he was initially distressed to learn the news. However, he acknowledged that it would probably be in her best interests, and they bade each other a highly emotional and tearful goodbye, but not before promising to write to each other every day.

He was visited daily by Thomas Wright, a well-known Manchester prison reformer. The two men grew very close, and the prisoner would share the contents of each day's letter from Martha with him, before throwing it on the fire. The prisoner would not discuss the children, other than to insist they had been murdered by Meller. He showed no remorse, and claimed that his defence should not have been based on the claim that he was insane, but that the killing of Meller had been justified. He wrote a lengthy petition to Queen Victoria, setting out the reasons why he had acted as he did, but decided against sending it. As his execution drew closer, he told Mr Wright that he would tell him how the children had died, but eventually declined to do so, saying only that they had not suffered, and he would take the secret to his grave.

Taylor was executed at noon, on Saturday, 13 September 1862, outside the walls of Liverpool's Kirkdale gaol. It was a double hanging, as he shared the scaffold with John Ward of Ashton-under-Lyne, who had shot a policeman to death. The crowd was estimated at one hundred thousand, and some of the poorest had walked from Ashton and Manchester to witness the spectacle. One thousand had slept in front of the gaol overnight, and four hundred had slept in the grounds of Warrington workhouse.

Thomas Wright was the first to walk out onto the scaffold, followed by Taylor and Ward, who was closely followed by William Calcraft, the hangman. The prison chaplain, who was reading the Burial Service, led the official party out. Ward threw his cap into the crowd as he walked towards the drop, and Taylor waved his hands and bowed to the crowd three or four times. Calcraft pinioned the men and then placed the white hoods over their heads, and drew the bolt. The crowd had been taunting Calcraft as he went about his business on the scaffold, and he now stood between the two suspended bodies and pulled his face in a grotesque grimace at the jeering spectators.

The bodies were cut down after one hour, and Taylor's beard was shaved off and a cast made of his face and head. In his pocket was a handkerchief, which his wife had given him at their final parting, and which she had asked him to have returned to her after the execution. This was removed and handed to Mr Wright who, as he had promised Taylor, sent it to her.

CHAPTER 3

The Hyde Road Rescue
1867

At about 3 am on the morning of 11 September 1867, a police patrol came across a group of four men, who were acting suspiciously, on Oldham Street, close to Manchester city centre. Two made off, but the remaining pair were detained and taken into custody, under the provisions of the Vagrancy Act, as they were thought to be about to break into a shop. The arrested men, who spoke with American accents and were found to have revolvers, gave their names as John White and Martin Williams. However, the police soon suspected that they were holding two members of the Fenian movement. Checks were made with members of the Irish police, who had been posted in Liverpool specifically to seek out members of this Irish nationalist organisation. Confirmation was soon received that the two prisoners were in fact thirty-six-year-old Colonel Thomas Kelly, and twenty-nine-year-old Captain Timothy Deasey. Kelly was a major figure in the organisation, and Deasey acted as his assistant. Their detention was authorised until 18 September, and on that date, Manchester was destined to be the setting for one of the Victorian age's most sensational crimes.

Formed to secure Irish independence, the Fenian movement recruited many Irish Americans in the mid 1860s, following the end of the American Civil War. Many American soldiers, of Irish descent, decided to put their military experience at the service of Ireland. At the war's end, many who had fought for the North and those who had worn the grey of the southern states, found common cause, and made their way across the Atlantic. Earlier, in 1867, a Fenian uprising had been crushed in Ireland, and Kelly and Deasey were amongst those who had escaped to the mainland, where they had intended to reorganise and continue their campaign. Kelly had in fact opposed the uprising, as he considered the organisation was ill-prepared, and not yet ready. This had not made him popular with some of his colleagues, but his arrest and detention was recognised as a body blow, for he was viewed as a brave man, a good organiser and a charismatic leader. If he could be rescued, it would bolster morale amongst the organisation's membership, and cause considerable embarrassment to the authorities.

Kelly and Deasey were held in Belle Vue gaol, and a friend by the name of Edward Shore arranged for the caterer who provided meals at the gaol, to cook special meals for his friends. Shore also arranged for the two prisoners to be legally represented. However, Shore, whose real name was Edward O'Meagher Condon, was the leader of the Fenians in the north of England, and he was also making other plans to assist his friends, as he was making arrangements for a spectacular rescue.

The van which transported prisoners between the gaol and the city's courts, took the same route every day. Shore found

Belle Vue gaol, to which Colonel Kelly and Captain Deasey were returning when they were rescued. Manchester Faces and Places

what he believed was the most suitable location for a rescue attempt, which was a railway arch on Hyde Road. It was not only a good spot to stop the van, but there was what appeared to be a good escape route across the railway line and out of Manchester. Shore had only a few days to find sufficient arms and volunteers to take part in the rescue. He obtained guns from sympathisers in Birmingham, and a group of about fifteen was selected from the many who had volunteered from Manchester's Fenian sympathisers.

Kelly and Deasey were brought before the magistrates at the city police court as arranged, and at this hearing, Inspector Williamson of the Metropolitan Police, formally identified Williams as Colonel Kelly, and White as Captain Deasey. The officer continued by advising the court that both had participated in the uprising a few months earlier, and he requested a remand for a further week, which the court agreed to. Kelly and Deasey were placed in a cell to await the arrival of the van, at 3 pm as usual, that would return them and a number of other prisoners to Belle Vue gaol. As the van arrived at the front of the court building, police officers noticed two men acting suspiciously, whom they suspected of being sympathisers of Kelly and Deasey. The officers rushed them, and although one escaped, the other produced a knife with which he attempted to stab one of the police officers. He failed to do so and was arrested: these two men were not part of the rescue plan.

Kelly and Deasey were handcuffed and placed in compartments to segregate them from the other prisoners, who sat in the corridor of the van, with Sergeant Brett of the Manchester police, who was armed with just his cutlass. The driver and seven other officers were sat on the outside of the van itself and another four officers followed in a cab: none of the officers carried any type of arms. The van began its three mile journey to the gaol, and it was uneventful until it reached the railway arch on Hyde Road.

What happened during the next ten or so minutes has been the subject of debate and controversy ever since. It is unlikely that a comprehensive and fully agreed version could ever have been given, even at the time: witnesses, be they civilians or police and prison officers were shown to be mistaken in some instances, and as will be seen, this was especially so in the case on one of the men eventually accused, named Maguire. The rescuers themselves gave varying accounts many years later, as the Fenian movement became embroiled in arguments, which led to its eventual demise. The account that follows is based on contemporary witness statements.

Despite the issues raised above, it is possible to describe in general terms what occurred as the prison van reached the railway arch, but filling in precise details is not easy. The first issue relates to the number of those who participated in the rescue attempt itself, as witnesses speak of numbers ranging from twenty to many more. These discrepancies probably stem from the fact that the planned assault on the van was widely known amongst the city's Fenian sympathisers, and many had come to the scene to watch, and probably joined in for brief spells, throughout the incident to assist during the rescue bid.

As the van approached, a group of men moved towards the middle of the road, taking out their revolvers as they did so. A tall man emerged from this group and raised his hand, whilst shouting for the driver to stop the van, and as he did so he fired his revolver into the air. Another man moved towards the van and shot both of the horses, preventing it from moving any further. The police officers on the van climbed off as there was little they could do, as they were all unarmed.

As the van was now unguarded, this enabled a group of rescuers to surround it, as their comrades held at bay the police and a number of civilians who were attempting to help the officers. Some of the rescuers climbed on to the van roof, which they tried to break through using a hammer, axe and large stones. One of the men put his gun through the ventilator flap of the door and was seen to fire his pistol, having been heard demanding that the keys be passed out to him. They were eventually handed to him through the flap and as he opened the door, a policeman was seen to fall out with a serious head wound.

A number of screaming women prisoners emerged from the van and ran away from the scene. A few moments later, Kelly and Deasey, still in handcuffs, came out and ran towards the railway line, as did many of those who had participated in the attack. They were pursued by several police officers and

The van is attacked as it reaches the railway arch on Hyde Road. The Illustrated Police News.

civilians, who bravely tried to help the police. A group of warders from Belle Vue gaol had by now arrived, having been alerted by a cabman, and they played a significant role in detaining many of those attempting to flee.

Allen, Larkin and Gold, the three men who were eventually singled out as having taken leading roles in the rescue, and who would pay with their lives. The Illustrated Police News

Several people were shot and suffered wounds, but there was to be just the one fatality. Indeed, from reading witness accounts a picture emerges of the attackers making efforts to avoid casualties if at all possible. In the immediate aftermath of the assault on the van, several police officers were of the opinion that many of the weapons were firing blanks. Furthermore, several of the leading participants, who were armed with loaded guns, were taken into custody by civilians and unarmed police and prison officers. However, they seem to have used their firearms to frighten their pursuers, rather than taking deliberate aim at people. One of those captured had two loaded revolvers, and as a group closed in to apprehend him, he simply fired his guns into the ground, before being disarmed. Nevertheless, loaded weapons were used, individuals were wounded, and a police officer was killed in the performance of his duty.

The police officer who had been mortally wounded was fifty-one-year-old Sergeant Charles Brett, whose home had been at 7 Wilson Street, off Oldham Road. It was unusual for an officer to be inside the van, and this was usually done so that the conversations of prisoners could be listened to, rather than as a guard.

At his inquest, a colleague, Constable George Shaw, who had been sat on top of the van became the first person to formally identify William Allen as the man who fired the shot into the interior of the van, which killed Sergeant Brett. Shaw described seeing Allen fire several shots warning people to keep away from the van. He then insisted that Allen had taken deliberate aim at the van with his pistol, before firing but he could not say whether this was at the keyhole and lock or through the ventilator flap. After a short time he heard a woman's voice from inside the van shout 'He's shot.' The van door then opened and Sergeant Brett fell out.

In response to a question from a jury member who asked whether the constable believed whoever fired the fatal shot was aware that there was an officer in the van, Constable Shaw thought that he would indeed have known. At this point, the coroner, Mr Herford, emphasised that whatever the answer to that question was, it should not affect the verdict, as an individual who fired a gun in such circumstances would be guilty of murder.

Sergeant Brett had been taken to the Royal Infirmary, where he was treated by Mr John R Woodcock, house surgeon, who was called as the next witness. He testified that the officer had been brought in at about 4.30 pm, unconscious, and obviously close to death, with a gunshot wound to the right eye: he died at 5.25 pm without having regained consciousness.

Mr Woodcock performed a post-mortem, and found a fracture in the roof of the right orbit, where the ball had entered the skull's cavity: a second fracture was found in the right side of the crown of the head, where the ball had exited the skull. There was an extensive laceration of the brain, between the two apertures. In conclusion, Mr Woodcock stated that in his opinion death had been caused from the injury to the brain, by the passage of the ball. The other half of his brain and all internal organs were in a healthy condition.

Mr Herford had noted that the deceased was a tall man, and he asked the doctor what direction the ball would have had to have taken if the sergeant had been stood erect in the van. Mr Woodcock replied that it would have had to have travelled upwards, at an angle of approximately forty-five degrees.

Sergeant Brett had been a much respected officer amongst his police colleagues, and at the city police court, where he had acted as dock officer. Furthermore, he had a reputation of treating the criminals in his charge with compassion and fairness: that he left a widow and three children, added to the sense of outrage in Manchester.

The police had arrested a number of suspects, many of whom had been detained at the scene of the rescue, and in the days that followed, they were held in the town hall, where they were lined up against the wall of a long corridor for several identity parades. This led to twenty-six accused appearing before the Special Commission, that was set up to try the case, which opened on 28 October 1867, before Mr Justice Mellor and Mr Justice Blackburn. The trial went ahead in Manchester despite defence lawyers arguing that it should be held in London, as feelings were running so high in the city at which the alleged crimes were said to have occurred.

Several of the accused were subsequently acquitted and seven received sentences of penal servitude, and those were: John Carroll (23), Charles Moorhouse (22), John Brannon (40), Thomas Scalley (22), Timothy Fetherstone (30), William Murphy (25) and Daniel Radden (25). The following year, William Darragh was convicted of purchasing the arms used in the rescue, in Birmingham, and was initially sentenced to death, although he was later reprieved.

Five of the accused were identified as having taken leading roles in the planning and execution of the rescue, and these were: William O'Meara Allen (19), Michael Larkin (30), Thomas Maguire (31), William Gould (30) and Edward Shore (26). Although tried under these names, Gould later identified himself as being Captain Michael O'Brien, who had served in the American civil war in the same regiment as Kelly, and Shore's true identity was also discovered.

A number of prosecution witnesses were called, and whilst none could provide an account of the incident from the beginning to end, each described a part of it that they saw. Each witness saw the events from different vantage points, and some arrived several minutes after it had begun.

Constable Joseph Yarwood had been sat with the van driver, and as they approached the railway arch he noticed the crowd that had assembled there. He saw Larkin shoot the horses in the neck, after which he fired at the van, but seemingly without taking deliberate aim. Gould came from the direction of the back of the van, and also shot at the horses. The witness later saw Allen with a revolver in each hand. Constable Shaw was also on the van, and identified Allen, Larkin, Gould and Shore as being in the group of attackers, and saw Allen firing at the van. Later, after Sergeant Brett's body had toppled out, he saw the same four men surround it, and drive away a number of the officers, with stones and revolvers.

Fellow officers gave corroborative evidence, including Constable William Carrington, who told the court that Allen had pointed two pistols at him, before shooting a civilian, Henry Sprosson in the foot. Detective Seth Bromley was on the van, and described being shot in the thigh by Allen, whom he later saw on the van roof trying to force it open with a stone that had been passed to him by Gould. Constable John Thomas identified Shore as playing a major role, and saw him throwing stones at the police. Constable Truman testified that Gould had fired a pistol at him, but that he had missed.

Several civilian witnesses were also called and provided damning evidence against the accused. Robert Patterson saw Allen trying to break into the van roof, and a little later saw him carrying two revolvers. He then saw him shoot through what he believed was the ventilator flap. He saw Kelly and Deasey emerge from the van, and heard Allen shout 'Ah Kelly, I'll die for you before I deliver you up!' As the other two ran off, Allen remained at the van for a time, threatening to shoot anyone who attempted to intervene. He provided no evidence against the others, save that he saw Maguire throwing stones. Another witness, George Pickup confirmed what the previous witness had said about Allen's role, and he also testified that he had seen Larkin carrying a hammer.

John Griffiths also described the extent of Allen's involvement, and added that he saw him shoot Sprosson in the foot. He had also seen Maguire at the scene, but had not seen him do anything specific. Twelve-year-old George Mullholland testified that he had heard Larkin threaten to kill the van driver, and had seen him pass a large stone to Maguire, who was on the van roof. The youngster had also seen Sprosson shot but could not say who had done it.

Other witnesses described the role played by Allen, including William Hulley, landlord of the nearby *Railway Inn*, who said that Allen had shot directly at him and his wife, after they had gone out to see what was happening. Only two more witnesses testified to seeing Maguire, and the first of these was Josiah Munn, driver of an omnibus that was held up at the arch. He insisted that he had seen him throw a stone at the driver of the prison van. Another witness was Henry Slack, a passenger on the omnibus, who testified that he had seen Maguire amongst the rescuers.

Henry Sprosson worked at St Matthew's Church on Hyde Road, and lived close to the railway arch. On hearing the commotion he had gone out to investigate. Police officers were asking the civilian onlookers to help them take back possession of the van. He decided to help, but as he moved forward someone in the crowd shouted 'Come back you fool.' He turned around and as he did so he felt the ball enter his foot, although he could not say who had shot him.

Inside the van a scene of terror was described by the women prisoners, Emma Halliday, Ellen Cooper, Frances Armstrong and the twelve-year-old boy prisoner, Joseph Parkinson. They described the van coming to a sudden stop, the shots and the sound of stones being thrown against the van, and not knowing what was happening added to their fear. The only individual who remained calm was Sergeant Brett. They described how he had peered out of the ventilator trap and exclaim 'Oh my God, it is those Fenians.' Then a stone came through the roof, which narrowly missed him.

A man's voice shouted through the door 'If you give us the keys we will let the two men go and do you no harm.' Brett replied 'Whatever happens, I will stick to my post to the last.' The sergeant was stood up at the door, looking through the flap, and a pistol emerged through it. Emma Halliday, who was sitting next to him, grabbed at the officer's clothing and pulled him downwards saying 'Oh Charlie, do come away, look there.' The pistol was then fired and the sergeant fell to the floor, mortally wounded. Emma testified that it was Allen who fired the shot, as she had seen him through the flap. Ellen Cooper testified that Allen had then shouted to them 'Get me the keys or I'll blow your brains out.' They did so, and when the doors were opened the women and the boy ran to the safety of Belle Vue gaol.

After leaving the van, Kelly and Deasey headed for the railway line, and made good their escape. They later reached America, where Deasey died in the 1880s. Kelly died in February 1905 after a career as a New York customs officer. However, some of their supporters who had assisted in the escape were not to be so fortunate.

According to Robert Patterson, Allen, Larkin and Gould followed Kelly and Deasey, and he heard Allen threaten to shoot any pursuers, and he saw him fire at one man. All three were eventually caught. A local grocer, John Knowles, on realising what was happening had gone into his house for his revolver before joining in the pursuit, and although he had shot at Allen he missed. Warehouseman, George Moorhouse, joined in the chase, and grabbed hold of Gould with the words 'My man, I think I've got you, and be hanged to you; we have thee all right.' He then chased Allen, who shot into the ground to warn him off, but Moorhouse was not to be deterred and he grabbed hold of him. The Fenian's revolvers were taken from him, and he was hit about the head with one of them, but he was protected from a vengeful crowd by the warehouseman, who made sure he was handed over to a police officer.

By this time, a number of gaolers had arrived from Belle Vue, and one of these was Joseph Howard. He saw Allen and Gould together, and was present when Larkin was detained in the nearby railway goods yard. He too was being assaulted by a number of his pursuers, but Howard took hold of him and handed him over to a police officer. Another gaoler, John Baxter took Gould into custody and again handed him over to a police officer.

The place and time of Maguire's arrest is not known but significantly it was not at the scene of the attack on the van. Shore, however, was arrested at about 5 pm, in Manchester by Constable Hirst and Sergeant Pears, despite briefly escaping from their custody. Upon being recaptured, Constable Hirst described being forced to hit him on the head with his baton.

The defence did not cross examine the prosecution witnesses to any great extent, other than to highlight some discrepancies. They began their case by arguing that they should be charged with manslaughter and not wilful murder. They based this on the argument that the detention of Kelly and Deasey had been wrongly authorised by the magistrates and they were therefore in custody illegally. They argued that if any individual so detained attempted to escape and in the process somebody was killed, the charge should be reduced to the lesser one of manslaughter. The two judges retired to consider this point, and returned thirty minutes later. Mr Justice Blackburn said that he and Mr Justice Mellor had given the matter some thought, and in their view there would only be some merit in the argument if the individual him or herself who had been illegally detained took the action the defence team had suggested. However, this was not the case if others took it upon themselves to attempt a rescue and murder was the appropriate charge in this case.

This having failed, the defence called alibi witnesses for three of their clients. Mary Flanagan, a governess, who claimed not to have known Gould previously, testified that she had seen him outside of a pub away from the scene at 3.50 pm, which would have made it impossible for him to have been at the arch at the time of the rescue. Mary O'Leary testified that at about the time of the attack on the van, she was travelling on an omnibus, and it had been bumped into by a cart, breaking one of its wheels. Gould was passing and spoke to a child that she knew.

Isabella Fee, a beerhouse keeper in Rochdale Road, and her son, both testified that Shore had been in their premises at the time of the attack, and had stayed for thirty minutes. They were supported by a tailor, Francis Kelly, who stated that he had been in the premises at the same time as Shore.

Several witnesses were called on behalf of Maguire. His sister, Elizabeth Fayden with whom he was staying, in Salford, testified that he did not get out of the bed on the day of the crime, until after 3.30 pm as he had been unwell. He had not left the house until almost 7 pm, and six neighbours testified that each had spoken to him between 3 pm and 5 pm on the day in question. Maguire was in fact a marine, who had only been home for a few days having been abroad for several years, and he had insisted since his arrest that he knew nothing of the Fenian movement and did not know where Hyde Road was.

Nevertheless, the jury found all five men guilty of the murder of Sergeant Brett, and when asked if they had anything to say, each protested his innocence. They were sentenced to death, but a problem immediately presented itself. In an unprecedented act, the members of the press who had been covering the trial, convinced of Maguire's innocence, immediately wrote to the Home Secretary, asking that he be pardoned. Despite fears that to agree to this unusual request, would undermine the case against the other four men, this was agreed to, and after spending a brief time in the condemned cell, Thomas Maguire was released and resumed his service in the marines.

When Shore's identity and American citizenship became known, his government petitioned for a reprieve. This was agreed to and his sentence was commuted to life imprisonment. He served eleven years after which he returned to his homeland and wrote an account of the rescue in the early twentieth century.

These developments had raised hopes that the three remaining prisoners would be reprieved, but this was not to be the case, and on the morning of 23 November 1867, they were amongst the last to be hanged in public.

The government was haunted by the fear of yet another rescue attempt, this time of the three condemned men, and so anyone walking the streets of Manchester on the eve of the executions would have thought that they were in a city under military occupation. The hangings were to take place at the New Bailey gaol in Salford, and the nearby line of the Lancashire and Yorkshire Railway was closed to traffic the day before and on the bridge, was camped a company of the 54th Regiment. Each man had forty rounds of ball in his pouch, and the rifles of the sentries were loaded. The volunteers kept guard in the central space in front of the scaffold until 2 am, when they were relieved by the special constables. The tension became more acute when it was learnt that Calcraft, the hangman, had received a threatening letter which read:

> *Sir, if you hang any of the gentlemen condemned to death at the New Bailey prison, it will be the worse for you. You will not survive afterwards.*

As the crowds began to assemble in front of the scaffold, which was on the outside wall of the prison, about thirty feet above ground level, the condemned men were spending their last night in the presence of three priests. Larkin, the only married man had said a tearful goodbye to his mother, wife and four children earlier that afternoon, but Allen had been refused permission to see Mary Anne Hickey, the girl he had hoped to marry.

Michael Larkin bids an emotional farewell to his mother, wife and children on the eve of his execution. The Illustrated Police News

Calcraft, the hangman prepares the condemned. The Illustrated Police News

The three men were awakened at 4.45 am, and attended mass at 5.30 am. They were pinioned whilst praying. At 8.02 am the prisoners, the priests, their guards, the mayor, prison governor and other officials, emerged into the prison courtyard, and climbed up the inside of the prison wall. At 7.58 am, soldiers had appeared on the ramparts, and on each side of the drop, and hidden from general view, was a platform holding soldiers, with loaded weapons drawn.

The black screen behind the gallows opened and the three men stood on the drop to a mixture of cries of derision and support from the assembled crowd. Gould approached Allen and shook his hand before kissing him on the cheek. Calcraft put the white cap over Allen's head, placed the noose around his neck, and repeated this with the other two men. Calcraft stepped back and drew the bolt. Calcraft had used three different lengths of rope for the men, and the longest was that used for Allen, who died instantaneously. However, Gould and Larkin suffered for some time afterwards, before being cut down at 9 am.

The rescue of Kelly and Deasey, the murder of Sergeant Brett, and the executions of Allen, Larkin and Gould, who became known as the 'Manchester Martyrs,' occurred almost

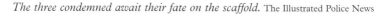

The three condemned await their fate on the scaffold. The Illustrated Police News

a century and a half ago. However, debate and controversy continues today. For instance, many believe that Allen did not fire the shot that killed Sergeant Brett. Many years later, one of the men originally selected as a member of the group of rescuers, named Peter Rice, who had escaped to America, claimed responsibility.

In 1897, a memorial to Allen, Larkin and Gould was erected in Moston Cemetery, and the foundation stone was laid by James Stephens, who had been leader of the Fenian movement in the 1860s. The three men are still remembered by the city's Irish nationalist supporters at an annual act of remembrance.

Sergeant Brett was buried in Harpurhey Cemetery, and his widow was awarded a pension for life by a grateful city.

The Right Reverend Monsignor Gadd, who attended Allen on the eve and morning of the execution. Shortly before the hanging, the priest placed his own silver crucifix around Allen's neck. He retrieved it after the execution, and kept it close to him for the rest of his life.
Manchester Faces and Places

CHAPTER 4

The Shudehill Stabbing
1869

If we need reminding of just how violent the streets of mid-nineteenth century cities could be, we need look no further than the stabbing of John Oldham and James McIntyre on the corner of Shudehill and Copperas Street close to Manchester city centre on Sunday, 31 January 1869, at a few minutes before midnight. Oldham would later die of his injuries, but McIntyre survived the savage assault, for which three Italians, all of whom were residents of Manchester, were arrested. They were twenty-four-year-old John Bernadotti, twenty-seven-year-old Joseph Retson and thirty-six-year-old Bartholomew Galgani.

Despite the lateness of the hour there were many people at this busy junction, amongst whom were the three Italians, linked arm in arm. They approached the other small group of men, Oldham, McIntyre and their companion James Burns. The two groups met, and one of the Italians was seen to stumble. Words were exchanged, and this minor fracas quickly escalated into a deadly encounter. As they struggled, witnesses saw the Italians draw knives, and Oldham was seen to fall to the ground, badly wounded, whilst McIntyre, who had also been stabbed, managed to make his way across the road to safety, and Burns avoided injury.

Constable Thomas Ashton was close by, and assisted by onlookers, he managed to detain Bernadotti and Galgani at the scene. Retson, who had left his cap at the scene, which was to link him to the crime, ran off, but he was arrested a short time later. Oldham received emergency medical treatment where he had fallen, from a Dr Paton, before being taken to the Royal Infirmary.

Bernadotti and Galgani were taken to Swan Street police station, where Inspector Thomas Hudson took charge of the

John Oldham is mortally wounded. The Illustrated Police News

case. Knives were found on both of them, and also on Retson, who was brought in about thirty minutes later. The hands of Bernadotti and Galgani were covered in blood, and Inspector Hudson, when later giving evidence in court, would describe them as appearing as though 'They had just been killing pigs.' The three men were detained overnight and on the following morning they were brought before the magistrates in the city police court. Having listened to the facts provided by the police, the court ordered that they be detained in custody until Thursday, 4 February, when further information on the condition of the stabbing victims would be given.

At the next hearing, Sergeant Gee advised the court that McIntyre was in a satisfactory condition, but it was unlikely that Oldham would survive, and a death bed statement had therefore been taken from him.

The unfortunate Oldham survived until the night of Friday, 19 February, and he made his statement before local magistrate

Alderman Crewdson, and also in the presence of the three accused. Oldham's statement must have been given in a highly charged atmosphere as victim and accused came face to face once again, and it read as follows:

About twelve o'clock last night I was at the corner of Copperas Street, going home, and saw three men coming towards me. They were talking and jostling one another. A tall man with a black moustache, took out of his right hand pocket something which shone like a knife. I believe it was a knife. He struck me with it as I passed him: I turned round, and was struck by a little man, who wore light trousers, upon the left shoulder. After the first named man had struck me, I felt that I was stabbed in the neck. I called out: my brother came and I pointed out to him my assailant. I know the man with the black moustache well: he lives in Stable Street, and is a maker of plaster of Paris figures. He is a foreigner. I fell upon being struck, and lost sight of the man: but directly afterwards, upon being lifted, I saw him in the custody of the police constable. The other man who struck me ran away, and I did not see him again. When the three men first approached me I stepped off the footpath to make way for them. I was sober. Two companions, James Burns and James McIntyre were with me. They came towards me when I called out, but I did not see them do anything. I am a confectioner, and occupy a passage next to where the man with the black moustache lives: and the tenant of the house where he lives has frequently wanted this passage from me. The three men, being now before me, I can positively say that the one who calls himself John Bernadotti is the man who struck me in the neck. Bartholomew Galgani keeps the house where Bernadotti lives, but I did not see him do anything. He did not strike me, and I cannot say that he is one of the three men whom I have spoken of as coming towards me upon the footway. I did see him after I had been picked up.

Oldham pointed directly at Bernadotti, and exclaimed 'This is the one.' Bernadotti replied 'I did not strike you did I?'

'Yes you did,' was the dying man's response as the three prisoners were led away.

Such statements have always been of huge importance in British law, and it certainly proved to be so in this case, as

THE MURDEROUS ASSAULT BY FOREIGNERS IN MANCHESTER.

DEATH OF THE WOUNDED MAN.

The man John Oldham, who was stabbed in an affray with foreigners (three of whom are in custody) in Manchester on the night of the 1st instant, died at the Royal Infirmary on Friday night. The deceased, in his dying deposition, which was taken before a magistrate a few days ago, stated that on the night in question, as he and two companions were turning the corner of Copperas-street, Shudehill, they met the three foreigners now in custody. They had no controversy whatever, but as they were all more or less the worse for drink they began to jostle each other on the footpath. One of the foreigners, named Bernadotte, a maker of plaster of Paris, whom the deceased knew, drew a knife and stabbed him in two places in the neck. The inquest was formally opened by the city coroner on Saturday and adjourned.

John Oldham's death is announced. Manchester Evening News

despite the crowd who witnessed the confrontation, nobody had actually seen the stabbings.

The inquest on John Oldham opened on Saturday, 20 February, but was adjourned so that a post-mortem could be performed by Mr T H Pinder, house surgeon at the Infirmary. At the resumed inquest on Saturday, 6 March, Dr Pinder described the deceased's wounds to the coroner and the jury. Oldham had been a healthy man, and there was a wound on the left side of his neck, which was three inches deep, an inch below the angle of the jaw, and which had cut the carotid artery: this had obviously been caused by a knife. There was another stab wound on the left shoulder blade, but this was not deep, and did not contribute to Oldham's death, which had been due to 'exhaustion consequent on repeated bleeding.'

Thus, the coroner's jury had the victim's testimony, and the post-mortem results, which confirmed the neck wound as being the most serious. In reaching their verdict, the jury seems to have accepted a degree of provocation, and they concluded that manslaughter was the most appropriate charge. They found that only Bernadotti and Retson were responsible, and they cleared Galgani of any responsibility.

Despite the findings of the inquest, all three of the accused were still held in custody awaiting their trial for wilful murder, which took place on Saturday, 13 March, before Mr Justice Brett at Manchester Assizes. They appeared before a different jury than that at the coroner's court, and in an attempt to ensure a fair trial, half of the jury members selected to hear the case were foreigners living in Manchester. The prosecution was led by Mr Hopwood; Mr Grimshaw and Mr Torr represented Retson and Galgani, and Mr Cottingham defended Bernadotti: all three defendants pleaded not guilty.

It is obvious from reading the proceedings of the trial, that in his opening submission, the prosecutor, Mr Hopwood presented the jury with an impeccably fair assessment of the issues that were relevant in this case. Having outlined the details of the original confrontation, he told the jury that they might find evidence to convict just Bernadotti of murder and the others of lesser charges, or they might think that all three should be convicted of manslaughter.

The jury heard Mr Pinder's findings, and the decision to arrange for Oldham to make his statement before Alderman

The coroner's jury reached a verdict that the trial jury would not fully agree with.
Manchester Evening News

THE ALLEGED MURDER BY ITALIANS IN SHUDEHILL. — At the Coroner's court last Saturday morning, the adjourned inquest on the body of John Oldham, one of the men stabbed in a row with three Italians on the 31st January, was held by the city coroner, Mr. Herford. The evidence given was merely a recapitulation of what has already appeared in the *Evening News*. A verdict of manslaughter was returned against Bernadotti and Reston, thus virtually acquitting Galgani, who is also in custody awaiting his trial for wilful murder.

Crewdson and the accused. The importance of the statement was clear to all of the lawyers, given that there was no other witness who could swear who was responsible for the fatal wound. There was thus a great deal of legal argument regarding its admissibility or otherwise, with the prosecution urging that it be admitted, and the defence representatives arguing against this.

Mr Cottingham argued that it should only be admissible if at the time it was made, the victim genuinely believed that death was imminent. If hope of survival was raised, as in the case of Oldham, who survived for almost three weeks after it was made, the statement became inadmissible. Several cases were cited, and this argument was supported by Mr Torr.

Mr Hopwood countered by quoting from the legal textbook *Russell on Crimes,* which suggested that it would be admissible, as the victim felt that death would follow quickly at the time of it being made, no matter what happened subsequently. In this particular case, it was noted that Oldham had urged Alderman Crewdson 'Be quick, or I shall die'.

These legal arguments lasted a considerable time and at their conclusion, the judge left to consult the senior and more experienced Mr Justice Lush. After doing so, he returned and agreed to admit the statement into evidence. This was on the grounds that the victim's carotid artery had been severed, and Dr Pinder had indicated that he might die at any minute after his admission to the Infirmary. There was thus little doubt that death at that time was considered to be inevitable and imminent. This, combined with Oldham's obvious awareness of his position, and fear that he would die soon, meant that he genuinely believed his own death was imminent when he made the statement. That he lingered until 19 February was not crucial in this case, as it could not disguise the perilous nature of his condition, and the view that Oldham himself took of it.

Mr Cottingham, however, persisted and asked the judge to delay admitting the statement to allow him the opportunity of taking the opinion to the Court of Criminal Appeal. The judge refused this application, and the death bed statement was read to the court by Mr G Thorpe, assistant clerk to the Manchester

Magistrates, who had been present when the deceased had made it.

After listening to the evidence of several witnesses to the confrontation, the jury listened to the closing arguments of the prosecution and defence representatives, followed by the judge's summing up. Mr Justice Brett believed that despite the persuasive statement made by the deceased, there had been an element of provocation, and he therefore advised the jury that a verdict of murder was not appropriate. They were thus to decide whether the accused were guilty of manslaughter only, and despite the findings of the coroner's jury, he believed that there was sufficient evidence against all three of the accused for them to consider.

The jury retired for ninety minutes and returned verdicts of guilty against all three of the accused. The judge told the prisoners it was a verdict with which he entirely agreed, as he was convinced that all three, who had knives in their possession, drew them, and each had been prepared to use them: in his opinion they had acted in concert. If there had not been some provocation, albeit of the smallest kind, they would have been convicted of murder and hanged.

He continued by stating that this type of violent crime was becoming all too common, especially in the north of England, and had to be dealt with severely. He described their behaviour as cowardly and as being both un-English and un-Italian.

Although convicted of manslaughter, he believed that their crime had been next to murder, and each was sentenced to twenty years penal servitude.

CHAPTER 5

The Prince's Club Shootings
1874

The Prince's Club, in the Cheapside district of Manchester, was one of the city's most exclusive gentleman's clubs, but in the late afternoon of Tuesday, 25 August 1874, it was the scene of a fatal double shooting. At a few minutes before 5 pm, Albert Rowley, the club porter, rushed into the nearby detective office, in a highly agitated state, and told the officers that two of the club's members had shot themselves in a duel. Such was the social

The Prince's Club, which was the scene of the murder and suicide. The Illustrated Police News

standing of the club's members, and the reputation of the club itself, that the porter had not considered any other explanation for such a tragedy.

The first police officer on the scene was Detective Inspector George Clayton, who quickly realised that a duel had not taken place. He had made straight for the room in which the shootings had occurred, where he found the club cook already there together with Frederick Arthur Barge. Inspector Clayton was immediately struck by the strong smell of powder as he noticed two bodies lying on the floor. Alexander Maclean lay on his left side, on the far side of the room, and there was a large pool of blood at his head. He appeared to have fallen off a chair, and there were writing materials and an unfinished letter on the table at which he had been sitting. The other man was Herbert Barge, who lay five feet away, and who was still alive with blood flowing from a head wound. His brother, Frederick, was desperately trying to stop the blood, but his efforts were in vain and Herbert died about fifteen minutes after the shooting.

Inspector Clayton realised immediately that both wounds had been caused by bullets, and noticed a revolver lay close to Herbert Barge's hand. A search by the officer and his colleague, Inspector Thompson, revealed evidence of three bullets having been fired: one had missed its target, and the other two were lodged in the brains of the two deceased. The two police officers had lifted Maclean's body and could find no other gun. By this time, Dr Birch, senior house surgeon at the Royal Infirmary, had arrived and confirmed that both men had died as the result of gunshot wounds to the brain. To the experienced police officers it was clear what had happened and that it was a case of murder followed by suicide: Herbert Barge had shot the other man, and then turned the gun on himself.

NOTICE TO NEWSAGENTS.

NEXT SATURDAY, SEPT. 5, 1874,

THE

ILLUSTRATED POLICE NEWS

Will contain a large Illustration of the

SHOCKING TRAGEDY AT PRINCE'S CLUB,

MANCHESTER.

From a Sketch made expressly.

GIVE EARLY ORDERS, AS A LARGE SALE IS EXPECTED.

OFFICE: 286, STRAND.

An early example of a sensational crime being used to promote the sale of a newspaper. The Illustrated Police News

Alexander Maclean is shot by Herbert Barge. The Illustrated Police News

The club was closed immediately, but as news of the crime spread a large crowd gathered outside, keen to hear of any developments in the case. Here was a case that did not occur in some back street slum, and did not involve members of the lowest social classes, but was committed in an exclusive club, and involved leading members of the city's business and social elite, as killer and victim. By the time the following morning's newspapers appeared speculation was rife as to what lay

The bodies are discovered. The Illustrated Police News

behind this fascinating and unusual crime. The insinuation that gambling debts might be the cause, was quickly dismissed after it was confirmed that Herbert Barge had never been seen to gamble or play cards. However, one theory that quickly took hold was that Herbert Barge suspected his victim of having inappropriate feelings for Mrs Barge, the wife he had married just a few weeks before, on 9 July 1874. What was not clear was whether there had been any justification in his believing this.

There was of course widespread interest in the inquest on both men, which was held in the club itself on the following day, Wednesday, 26 August, for which a jury comprising ten merchants, one banker, and an insurance agent was selected. It was held before the city coroner, Mr Herford, in one of the club's largest rooms. Police officers were placed at the club's main entrance to ensure that the large number of people, who had gathered outside did not force their way in and disrupt proceedings.

Both families involved in the tragedy were legally represented at the hearing. Mr Addison represented the Barge family, and Mr Gouldthorp appeared on behalf of the Macleans.

The first witness was Frederick Barge, brother of Herbert, whom he described as having been a twenty-nine-year-old merchant with interests in trade with South America, and the brothers were business partners, in their company, Messrs T Barge & Bros, commission agents and shipping merchants, of Brown Street. The witness lived in Buxton, and the previous day had gone to the club to try and book a room for the night, only to be told that they were all occupied. On entering the club he had met his brother, who had seemed to be in a rather agitated state of mind. They exchanged pleasantries as they made their way up the stairway. Frederick went into the lavatory to wash his hands, whilst Herbert continued up the stairs. A short time later, Frederick heard three shots fired in rapid succession. As he reached the stairs, he encountered one of the billiard markers, who called out, 'Your brother and Mr Maclean have shot each other.'

Frederick made his way to the room in which the shots had been fired, where he found his brother lying on his back, with a pistol in his hand. He lingered for about fifteen minutes, during which time the witness tried in vain to save him, as he had watched the blood flow from the head wound. He advised the court that he had seen his brother, accompanied by his wife at their office, on Monday, the day before the shooting, and both Herbert and his sister-in-law had seemed in good spirits.

The coroner asked about his brother's usual state of mind. Frederick described him as having been depressed during the previous eight or nine months, and this had manifested itself in what he described as 'a peculiar reserve towards old friends, against whom he had no cause whatever of resentment.' Also he had been in a 'gloomy tone of mind, always imagining the worst, and regularly anticipating gloomy events.' When Frederick had asked him why he felt this way, Herbert had replied by stating that he considered himself to be 'thoroughly bad.' Frederick had told his brother that this was absurd as he was the opposite in character.

Furthermore, during this period, his brother had become intensely pious, and prayed a great deal. When he did so he would adopt what Frederick described as a peculiar position, as he would lie in a prostrate position and extend his arms. Frederick had been aware that there were two pistols at Herbert's home, and in response to the coroner, he stated that he did not consider his brother to have been of sound mind. He confirmed that he had received a letter from his brother, which had arrived through the mail that very morning, which the coroner read out to the court:

St Mary's Gate, Manchester, August 24 1874
My dear Fred, - I implore your pardon for what I am going to do. I cannot bear longer my awful thoughts. I have not a soul to blame in the world for what I am about to do but my own self. This is a fearful end. Believe me my poor brother.

Yours Herbert.

Inspector Clayton told the court of being called to the crime scene, and what he had discovered there. He was followed in the witness box by Albert Rowley, the club porter. He told the court that on the previous day, Herbert Barge had arrived at the club, by cab, at some time between 1.30 pm and 3 pm. On entering the front hall, he immediately asked 'Is Mr Maclean in?' The witness advised him that he was not, but that he was expected at about 5 pm, as he had booked a room for the night. Herbert Barge made his way upstairs to the billiard room, where he was seen to shake hands and chat with several club members, before taking a cigarette from the billiard marker. He came back downstairs and stood for several minutes on the front steps of the club, smoking his cigarette as he looked up and down the road, as though waiting for someone. He then got back into his cab, which drove off.

At 4.40 pm, Frederick Barge arrived at the club, and was attempting to book a room for the night when his brother returned. The porter then watched the two of them make their way upstairs. A few moments later, the butler shouted down to the porter on behalf of Herbert Barge, to ask if Mr Maclean had arrived. He had arrived a little time earlier, and the porter knew that he was in the habit of writing letters at this time of day, but he was not sure which room he was in. The porter, followed by Herbert Barge, looked for him in the reading room and billiard room, before locating him in the smoking room.

On being told that Mr Maclean was alone, Herbert walked passed the porter into the smoking room. The porter saw Mr Maclean rise from his chair as if to shake hands with the visitor, but the door then closed. As he walked back to his desk, Albert was telling the billiard marker that Mr Barge had seemed to be under the influence of alcohol, when suddenly there were three shots fired in rapid succession, coming from the direction of the smoking room.

Next to give evidence was Abraham Rosson, a gunsmith, whose shop was on Market Street in the city centre. Herbert Barge had called at his shop at about 10.30 am on the previous day. He had told the gunsmith that he was about to embark on an overseas trip and wanted a gun that would 'shoot quick' to take with him. He paid for a muzzle loader and left the premises, saying nothing more.

The next witness was cabman Joseph Johnson, who had picked up Herbert Barge shortly before 4 pm on Monday, 24 August, in St Anne's Square, the day before the shooting. He had asked to be taken to Prestwich, and once the cab had arrived there he ordered the cabman to stop at a spot from which it was possible to see a particular house. Herbert told the cabman that the house belonged to Mr Maclean, and he asked him to keep watch for a man or woman either entering or leaving the premises. After forty-five minutes, during which time there were no arrivals or departures, his fare had asked to be taken to his own home near to Kersal Bar. When pressed by the coroner, the witness stated that he had been given no reason for the request to keep watch on the house. He did not think that Herbert Barge had been drunk but he had 'looked queer in the eyes.'

Edwin Coathupe, Deputy Chief Constable of Manchester, was the next witness to be called. He advised the coroner and jury that Herbert Barge had called at the police office during the morning of Monday, 24 August, asking for a private interview. The coroner had to prompt the officer to continue, to which the witness responded by asking, 'Must I state the conversation we had?' The coroner replied, 'I think you must, and I will judge whether there is anything objectionable in it.' The witness continued by stating that Herbert Barge had asked if a police officer could be provided to watch a man and woman.

The witness told Herbert this would not be possible, but he was prepared to recommend a retired officer, former Inspector John Buckley. He was called as the next witness and confirmed that Herbert had visited him at 11.45 am on Monday, 24 August. The deceased had given no further details of who was to be watched, or for what reason, as the former police officer turned the job down.

Mr Addison had arranged for Dr Frank Renaud, who had been consulted by Herbert some months previously, to attend the inquest, and the coroner agreed to hear his evidence. The doctor had seen the deceased on three or four occasions in the previous June and July, as he had stated that he had been feeling very nervous, could not sleep, and was oppressed with remorse. Dr Renaud, a highly respected Manchester doctor, was firmly of the opinion that his patient was of unsound mind.

Before retiring to consider their verdict, the jury members inspected the bodies of the two men, which had been laid out in line with the then custom. They very quickly reached their verdicts: whilst in a state of temporary insanity, Herbert Barge wilfully murdered Alexander Maclean, and then committed suicide whilst in a state of unsound mind. The foreman added that the jury members wished to express their displeasure with some of the local press, which had insinuated that the motive was jealousy, due to there having possibly been an affair between the murderer's victim and wife. The coroner concurred, as did Mr Addison, who insisted that there was absolutely no truth in the rumour. Frederick Barge insisted that his sister-in-law and Mr Maclean had only ever met once. This had been an area not explored by the coroner, who no doubt considered that there was no need to do so. It may well have been that the rumours were groundless, but it is clear from the witnesses who saw Herbert Barge in the days preceding the shootings, that he was probably under the delusion that there was such an affair going on.

At 5 pm the victim's body was removed by his family, and two hours later the perpetrator's kinfolk took his body away. The club remained closed until the following day, but curious crowds continued to gather outside throughout the night, which led to the police having to disperse them.

Dr Frank Renaud, a leading Manchester physician, who attempted to help Herbert Barge. Manchester Faces and Places

Alexander Maclean was buried at Prestwich parish church on Friday, 28 August, and the funeral was attended by many family members and friends. The cortege left the family home mid-morning, by which time Prestwich wakes should have begun. In Lancashire towns, the wakes were held over a few days each year, and were marked by much drunkenness and raucous behaviour. However, Alexander Maclean was a well known and widely liked member of the local community, and as a mark of respect, the villagers postponed their revels until after he had been buried.

On the morning of Monday, 31 August, there was a much quieter funeral for Herbert Barge. The cortège left the family home at Kersal Bar and made its way to All Saints Church in Stand, where this troubled man was interred in the family vault with his late parents.

CHAPTER 6

The Gorton Abortion Case
1875

At 11 pm on Monday, 15 March 1875, Mr Marshall, the stepfather of twenty-six-year-old confectioner, Margaret McKivett, called on Mr J L Fletcher, surgeon, at 2 Sydnall Street off Hyde Road. He advised the doctor that Margaret had been suffering stomach pains for the past few days, but her condition had deteriorated rapidly that day. As the men made their way through the dark streets, the doctor asked why he had not been sent for earlier. Mr Marshall replied that Margaret and her mother had both felt that she would recover, and that it would not be necessary to trouble the doctor.

Upon his arrival at Margaret's shop at 172 Hyde Road, it was immediately obvious to Dr Fletcher that Margaret was close to death, and that there was little that could be done, other than try and ease the pain. In the absence of any information from Margaret or the Marshalls, the doctor diagnosed inflammation of the bowels as the problem. What the doctor was not told was that earlier that day Margaret had suffered a miscarriage, nor was he aware of the circumstances that had led up to it.

Dr Fletcher was sent for again the following morning, and on reaching the shop was advised that Margaret had died at 5 am. Having confirmed that she was dead, Dr Fletcher indicated that he would be seeking a post-mortem. However, he was persuaded to abandon this idea after the Marshalls suggested it would be too upsetting for them. Instead, he issued a death certificate giving the cause as 'derangement of a portion of the intestines.'

However, police soon received anonymous information that there was more to Margaret's death than initially thought. It was not long before their enquiries led them to the chemist

The City Police Court, where Alfred Heap first appeared to face the charge of murder. Manchester Faces and Places`

shop owned by forty-one-year-old Alfred Thomas Heap, at 156 Gorton Lane, West Gorton, above whose doorway was a sign proclaiming him to be a 'SURGEON', although he was not qualified to practice as such.

Heap was well known to the police, and following their preliminary enquiries, they believed they had sufficient evidence to arrest him for the murder of Margaret McKivett. He was brought before the city police court on Thursday, 18 March. Police Inspector Standley confirmed that he had arrested the prisoner at 10 pm the previous evening on suspicion of murder, having performed an illegal abortion by means of inserting a sharp instrument into Margaret's womb. The operation had gone horribly wrong and as the unfortunate young woman's body lay in her shop, a post-mortem was being arranged. Heap was remanded in custody until 19 March, and, meanwhile, enquiries continued into the circumstances surrounding Margaret's death.

At his second court appearance he was represented by his solicitor, Mr E S Bent. The prosecution was conducted by Mr W Cobbett of Messrs Cobbett, Wheeler and Cobbett. In establishing their case against the accused, the prosecution called nineteen-year-old Sarah Ann Mottram, Heap's sister-in-law, who lived in Russell Road off Hyde Road. Sarah testified that she had seen Margaret on Thursday, 11 March at the home of Heap's estranged wife, who was a midwife, in Queen Street. Margaret had asked for Mrs Heap, but she had died the previous day. On the following day, Margaret had approached Sarah and asked her to contact the prisoner on her behalf. Sarah did so and a meeting was arranged for later that day, at Margaret's shop, where Sarah described seeing the pair deep in conversation in the kitchen. A few minutes later, Margaret left, saying she was going to Heap's shop.

Heap and the witness remained in Margaret's shop, and thirty minutes later, his housekeeper, Julia Ann Carroll arrived and told him that 'A party was waiting at home.' Heap left by the back door and made his way home together with Julia. Later evidence was to confirm that Margaret's mother, Mrs Marshall waited at Heap's premises whilst the abortion was performed, and at one point she became very distressed to find her daughter in a terrible condition. This led Julia to have to shout to her 'Don't make a noise. If a policeman was to hear you, he would arrest Mr Heap, thinking he had done something wrong.' Indeed, Julia Ann Carroll was at one stage arrested as an accessory, but was released after a brief time.

Sarah described Margaret returning home with her mother having left Heap's premises. She had seemed very ill and went to bed immediately.

Mr Cobbett next called Jane Draper, who was Margaret's shop assistant. She told the court that at about 11 am on Monday, 15 March, Margaret asked her to call on the prisoner with an urgent message to come and see her as she was extremely poorly. Heap arrived a few minutes later in a very drunken state, and made his way to Margaret's bedroom. After a brief time Jane heard Margaret cry out 'Don't,' to which Heap replied 'You are not going to make a die of it this time.' Heap left and on reaching Margaret's room Jane found her lying on the bed, covered in blood.

Mr Cobbett advised the court that the sharp instrument believed to have been used by Heap in performing the abortion, had been found. Heap was then remanded in custody to await his appearance at Liverpool Assizes, where he would stand trial for his life. This decision was made before the results of the post-mortem and inquest were known, as there was a great deal of circumstantial evidence against him.

The inquest was held on Wednesday, 24 March before Mr Herford, the city coroner. Details of the post-mortem were provided by Mr T Jones, Pathological Registrar at the Royal Infirmary. The post-mortem confirmed that Margaret had died after a sharp instrument had been inserted into her womb to procure an abortion, and the coroner's jury quickly concluded that Margaret had been murdered by Heap. The jury also censured Margaret's mother, Mrs Marshall, for what they termed 'gross concealment' as they seemed to believe that Margaret might have survived had medical assistance been called for earlier.

The trial took place at Liverpool Assizes on Friday, 2 April, with Mr West QC and Mr Jordan leading the prosecution and Mr Foard and Mr Warr acting for the defence. The prosecution evidence that had been presented at the initial hearings was repeated, and the trial jury was also advised that Margaret had borrowed a sovereign from Jane Draper to pay for the abortion, which had been insisted on by Mrs Marshall, as the baby's father was thought to be one of Margaret's uncles, which compounded the scandal already facing the family.

Mr West told the jury that the prosecution would not accept a manslaughter verdict. If the jury was convinced that Heap had deliberately set out to perform an abortion and in so doing had killed Margaret, he was as guilty as if he had intended to kill her. It was 'murder or nothing'.

The defence team resisted their client's wish to try and implicate his late wife, as the evidence against him was overwhelming. Instead they attacked the prosecution's insistence for a murder conviction, by highlighting the fact that he had not set out to kill Margaret. They drew a distinction between someone setting out deliberately and with premeditation to kill, and the actions of their client. Their closing argument was that 'If it is murder or nothing, then it is nothing'.

In his summing up the judge advised the jury that they could in fact bring in a verdict of manslaughter, but only if they believed that the prisoner had not intended to perform an abortion, but had for instance, only meant to examine her and offer some advice. If they felt he was not intending to terminate the pregnancy a manslaughter verdict would be acceptable.

The jury retired for ten minutes before returning with an inevitable verdict of guilty of murder, but they added a strong recommendation for mercy. The judge put on a black cap and before passing sentence told the prisoner

THE HYDE ROAD MURDER.

SENTENCE OF DEATH.

LIVERPOOL SPRING ASSIZES.

CROWN COURT.— TO-DAY.

Alfred Thomas Heap, described as "a surgeon," was charged with the wilful murder of Margaret M'Kivett, at Manchester, on the 12th of March.

Mr. West, Q.C., and Mr. Jordan appeared for the prosecutor; Mr. Foard and Mr. Ware defended.

Mr. West, in a lengthy opening statement, recapitulated the particulars of the offence with which the prisoner was charged.

Evidence similar to that given before the Magistrates and reported in the *Evening News* was given, and the case is proceeding.

The case appeared to excite great interest in the court, and we may briefly recapitulate the facts. Deceased occupied a confectioner's shop in Hyde-road, and finding herself *enceinte* she accompanied her mother on the morning of the 13th to prisoner's shop, and saw Heap himself. While her mother waited below, she underwent some operation at the hands of the prisoner, the effect of which was to render her insensible. On recovering, she met, Heap at a beerhouse, and paid him £1 On arriving at her home she was taken ill and continued to get worse until the morning of the 18th, when Heap called and after jeeringly telling her she mustn't "do a die" treated her in such a manner that death ensued the same day. He was now indicted for wilful murder.

Sarah Ann Mottram, Sarah Ann Marshall, and Mr. J. L. Fletcher having given evidence the case for the Crown closed, and the defence was then heard.

Heap was eventually convicted and sentenced to death.

Heap's trial took place at the Liverpool Spring Assizes, where he was convicted and sentenced to death. Manchester Evening News

that he took note of the jury's comments, but added that the verdict was one that he fully agreed with. Furthermore, he could now reveal information not known to the jury. This was that Heap's current offence was aggravated by the fact that he had 'Not only beforetime practised similar acts of wanton destruction of children before they came to birth, but that you have already been convicted of an offence of that kind'. The judge was referring to a conviction in August 1868 for attempting to procure an abortion on Sarah Lunn by means of a sharp instrument, for which he was sentenced to five years penal servitude.

The judge, however, did not inform the court that the prisoner had also stood trial for the murder of a woman in similar circumstances to those of the current case, in 1867, but had been found not guilty. This history, and Heap having continued to act in a brazen manner perhaps explains the authorities' antipathy towards him. This was to continue as determined efforts were made to save him from the gallows.

SOUTH LANCASHIRE ASSIZES.

SALFORD HUNDRED.

CROWN COURT, YESTERDAY.

(Before Mr. Justice Hannen.)

THE GORTON ABORTION CASE.

Alfred Thomas Heap, 34, was indicted for having, at Gorton, on the 1st May, attempted, by means of an instrument, to procure the miscarriage of Sarah Ann Lunn. Messrs. Leresche and Addison prosecuted; and Mr. Torr defended the prisoner.—The case occupied the Court several hours, but the evidence was wholly unfit for publication.—The prisoner was found guilty.

The Judge, in passing sentence, said the prisoner had been convicted upon evidence which satisfied his mind, as it had done that of the Jury, that he was guilty of the crime imputed to him. He (the prisoner) had made use of the small amount of medical knowledge which he had been able to pick up for a most infamous purpose, and he (the Judge) had no doubt that the prisoner had long carried on a trade which had attracted to him unhappy girls who wanted assistance in the trouble brought upon themselves by the gratification of evil passions. The prisoner was one of the most mischievous persons in the community, and he felt it to be a duty to pass upon him a sentence which would remove him for some time from the scene of his wicked operations. The sentence of the Court was that he be kept in penal servitude for a period of five years.

In August 1868, Heap had been sentenced for performing an abortion on another young woman, named Sarah Ann Lunn.
The Manchester Guardian

Heap was taken to Liverpool's Kirkdale gaol to await his fate. On Wednesday, 7 April he was visited by his fourteen-year-old son, his nephew, and two lady friends, who had found him to be calm, considering the situation he was in. Two days later his execution was fixed for Monday, 19 April at 8 am. Nevertheless, his friends were still hopeful of a reprieve, and by 9 April, three separate petitions had been circulated, including one that had been signed by four thousand residents of the Gorton area. Amongst the signatories were thirty local clergymen. Heap's solicitor, Mr Bent, later forwarded these petitions to Mr Cross, the Home Secretary.

THE CONDEMNED CONVICT AT KIRKDALE.

Yesterday, Alfred Thomas Heap, formerly druggist at Gorton Brook, who was sentenced to death at the Liverpool Assizes, last week, for the murder of Margaret M'Kivett, of Manchester, was visited by his son, his nephew, and two lady friends, who found him devoting the hours remaining between him and death to earnest prayer and supplication. Although he seems to feel his position, his demeanour is calm and unflinching.

THE CONDEMNED MAN ALFRED HEAP.

Up to a late hour last night no reprieve had been received at Kirkdale Gaol, Liverpool, for the condemned convict Alfred Thomas Heap. Should no reprieve arrive beforehand, the unfortunate man will be executed at eight o'clock on Monday morning within the precincts of the gaol. None of his relations or friends visited him yesterday. Mr. E. S. Bent had interviews yesterday with Mr. Bright, M.P., and Mr. W. R. Callender, M.P., in reference to the convict's case; and Mr. Callender has presented to the Home Secretary a memorial signed by some of the jury empanelled on the trial, in favour of a commutation of the sentence.

THE CONDEMNED MAN ALFRED HEAP.

Up to last night no reprieve had arrived at Kirkdale Gaol, Liverpool, for Alfred Thomas Heap; the man sentenced to death at the late assizes for the murder of Margaret M'Kivett, at Manchester. The culprit attended divine service yesterday, and seems to fully realise the awful position he is in. None of his relatives have visited him since Wednesday last, and should the capital sentence be carried into effect the execution will take place at eight o'clock next Monday morning.

Following another visit to the prison, Heap's relatives and friends found him to be hopeful of a reprieve, but resigned to his fate. He was spending much of his time in prayer and regularly attended services in the prison chapel. Meanwhile, Mr Bent continued his efforts to save his client's life and on Saturday, 17 April he met with two local MPs, Mr Jacob Bright and Mr W R Callender, and the latter agreed to present a letter to the Home Secretary, signed by several of the jurors at the trial, who favoured a reprieve.

Between sentence and execution or commutation of sentence, the press regularly reported on the condition of the condemned and his visitors.
Manchester Evening News

Many individuals also wrote to the Home Secretary and one such letter, from William Coleman of 59 Dale Street, Hulme, which was written on the day following the verdict and sentence, encapsulates the significant issues raised by the case:

Dear Sir – I beg to draw your attention to the case of Alfred Thomas Heap, who was tried at the Liverpool Assizes yesterday for murder and sentenced to death. I enclose a report of the trial.

I do not know the prisoner, neither have I sympathy for him in the crime he committed, but I do think that the laying down of the law that it was a case of murder or nothing is stretching the law in this particular instance. There seems such a difference between a man trying to procure an abortion to a consenting party, and that act resulting in death, than in a case where one man maliciously kills another; and I was not surprised that the jury, having the law laid down that it was a case of murder or nothing should, in bringing in a verdict of guilty, recommend the prisoner to mercy. The judge held out no hope to the prisoner, but I think it is a case in which capital punishment ought not to be inflicted, and I hope you will advise Her Majesty to grant a commutation of the sentence – I am sir, yours truly.

The Home Secretary's reply was sent on 17 April, just two days before the planned execution date, and held out little hope for the condemned:

Sir – Mr Secretary Cross having carefully considered your application on behalf of Alfred Thomas Heap, I am directed to express to you his regret that there is no sufficient ground to justify him, consistently with his public duty, in advising Her Majesty to comply with the prayer thereof, - I am sir, your obedient servant.

Also on Saturday, the scaffold was erected in its traditional location, the north-east corner of the gaol yard. On the following day, Sunday, 18 March, during the late afternoon, William Marwood the executioner arrived at the gaol.

On the Sunday, Heap attended two services, and at one of them he asked the prison chaplain, Reverend O F Piggott to address the other prisoners on his behalf, with the following:

It is the last day I shall be amongst you, and it will be a benefit to some to say that through true repentance and faith in Jesus I have made my peace with God, though the Devil causes me terror at times. Drink has been the cause of my committing many of these sins, which otherwise would not have been committed. I hope you will take warning.

Heap retired to bed at midnight and slept soundly for several hours. He rose at 6 am and made his way to the chapel, where he received communion with Robert Brewer, the gaol schoolmaster, and William Latham, governor of the Home for Discharged Prisoners, both of whom had been his constant companions in Kirkdale.

He later breakfasted before marching to the pinioning room. At a few minutes before eight the prison bell began to toll and the members of the press who were allowed to attend executions since their abolition in public in 1868, were ushered into the gaol yard. At 8 am precisely, Heap and those accompanying him, including Mr Hyslop, the chief warder, Major G E Leggatt, the governor, together with the under-sheriff, and the warders escorting him, walked across the yard, towards the scaffold. Throughout his time at Kirkdale, staff had been impressed by his calmness and great strength of character. His courage did not let him down now, for he maintained his composure as he walked up the steps of the scaffold, and at one point calmly looked up at the rope dangling from the beam.

On reaching the drop, he positioned himself and listened intently as Reverend Piggott exclaimed 'Oh Lord, be with him, we most humbly beseech Thee', the bolt was drawn and Heap took what was known as the 'long drop', that is one of more than five feet.

Later, Reverend Piggott revealed that Heap had made a full confession to Margaret's murder, although he insisted that he had not intended to kill her. However, this was not quite the end of the affair.

Throughout the whole of Monday, the day of the execution, after it had become clear that there was to be no reprieve, restive groups of people began to gather around the Gorton district. As the day progressed so the crowds grew until it was estimated that by the afternoon there were several thousand people there. Their focus was the shop owned by the Marshalls, and the thoroughfares around the premises were blocked. Omnibuses could not complete their journeys, and shopkeepers closed their premises early in the day. A section of the crowd began to bang on the shutters of the Marshalls' shop, with large sticks, but no doubt sensing there may be trouble they had left for Southport.

The police were there in large numbers to ensure there were no breaches of the peace. Many local inhabitants clearly felt strongly that Heap, despite his crime, should not have hanged, and felt that Mrs Marshall, in particular was to blame for his fate, and furthermore she had some responsibility for the death of Margaret. For instance, it was felt that she may have pressured her daughter into having the abortion, and also she was responsible for the delay in Dr Fletcher being called to treat her.

However, this was not necessarily the unruly mob described by the police and the press, bent on violence and destruction of property. For instance, there was an effigy of Mrs Marshall, and an attempt was made to set it alight but this was thwarted by the police; it had been arranged for a local band to attend the scene, but their appearance was fleeting and at a distance, because of the large number of people gathered in the neighbourhood, which meant they could not reach the Marshalls' shop. These are the hallmarks of 'rough music', to which the crowd had hoped to subject the unfortunate Mrs Marshall. This was a centuries-old tradition amongst working class people. It was a highly

THE HYDE-ROAD MURDER.
SINGULAR SCENE IN THE NEIGHBOURHOOD.
Last evening the news of the actual execution of Heap for the murder of the woman M'Kivett created intense excitement among the lower classes resident in the neighbourhood of Hyde-road and Gorton Brook. For days past every taproom has witnessed discussions as to the hardship of hanging the man for what was called an "accidental murder," whatever that may be, and last night the "rough" element recognised the fact that a favourable opportunity had arrived for indulging in the display of their customary rowdyism. Sympathy with the "unfortunate" Heap and indignation against Mrs. Marshall, mother of the murdered woman, and the chief witness at the assizes, were the pretexts for the after proceedings, but there can be little doubt that the mob which began to assemble between six and seven o'clock in the neighbour-

The execution of Alfred Heap was controversial, especially in Gorton where his neighbours protested at the decision. Manchester Evening News

ritualistic procession led by a band, who played loud raucous music, and in which an effigy was paraded outside the home of an individual who had behaved against the norms and customs of the neighbourhood, by possibly behaving in an immoral or otherwise unacceptable manner. The crowd would bang pots and pans and the noise could be deafening and frightening. Despite its unpleasant nature, there was rarely any direct contact, violence or damage to property when 'rough music' was performed. It was dying out by the close of the nineteenth century, but it survived in some districts until the early twentieth century, and would occasionally be heard.

Despite the large numbers of people present, and the level of anger they felt, it is noticeable that the police had no trouble in controlling the crowds, which had dispersed by 9 pm, without an arrest being made.

The neighbourhood's response to Heap's execution probably reflected the ambivalence with which the man himself and his activities were perceived within the community. He had conducted his business openly and few in the area could not have been aware of what the sign 'SURGEON' meant, and how he supplemented his income as a chemist. He had been responsible for death, injury and misery on a relatively large scale, but in an age when a single working class woman with sole care of a baby would usually find herself facing shame, ostracism, poverty and the workhouse, his services had probably been used by many in the area.

CHAPTER 7

The Ancoats Tragedy
1886

After stabbing his wife Matilda to death in their house at 3 New Street, Ancoats on 11 May 1886, Thomas Donohue immediately turned the knife on himself and inflicted wounds from which he later died. As details of the relationship of the fifty-six-year-old Donohue and his wife who was thirty years his junior emerged, it seemed that this was a tragic but typical example of a violent husband murdering his wife and then committing suicide. However, as subsequent and dramatic events were to reveal, this was an extremely unusual case.

Donohue, who managed a provisions shop owned by his son Denis in Butler Street had married Matilda, a local factory girl, fourteen months earlier. Until then she had lived with her parents, together with her illegitimate child. Donohue was aware of this and was said to be under the impression that the child's father had left the country. However, some weeks prior to the murder he had been told that Matilda had recently been seen in the company of her former suitor.

This had upset Donohue and had placed a great strain on their relationship to such an extent that he threatened to kill Matilda. Fearing for her safety, she left him and returned to her parents' home at 19 Garrick Street on 6 May. This was not the first time she had left her husband, and on a previous occasion she had done so for more than a month after he had badly beaten her.

On the morning of 11 May, Donohue made his way to his in-laws' house to attempt to persuade Matilda to return home with him. Initially she refused as she no doubt continued to be frightened of him, but he persisted for several hours. He seemed genuinely remorseful and was very persuasive. Eventually, at two o'clock in the afternoon, Matilda agreed to return home with him. Her sister, Sarah Ellen, remained concerned for Matilda's welfare, and decided to accompany the couple as they made their way to New Street.

During the journey Donohue and Matilda were mainly silent, but at least Sarah Ellen believed that the tension had lessened, as the couple seemed at ease with each other. Upon reaching home all three went inside, and he asked Matilda to light a fire. This she did, after which he suggested that she go upstairs and change her dress. Again she did as he suggested and after about two minutes, he left his sister-in-law and followed his wife upstairs.

A few minutes later Matilda screamed out 'Sarah Ellen, he is murdering me.' Her frantic sister ran upstairs and on finding the bedroom door fastened, she bravely burst into the bedroom to be confronted by a horrific sight.

Sarah Ellen tries desperately to save her sister's life, but could not prevent Thomas Donohue from killing her. The Illustrated Police News

Donohue and Matilda were both standing, and he was holding her with his left arm. She was covered in blood and in his right hand, he held a large butcher's knife, with which he was stabbing her. Showing great courage, Sarah Ellen managed to pull her sister from his grasp and made for the stairs hoping to escape. Matilda passed out at the top of the stairs and fell down them, dragging her sister with her. As both women fell the assailant followed them, still brandishing the butcher's knife.

Sarah Ellen's screams attracted the attention of a young man named William Duxberry, who was passing the house, and who sought out a police officer. He found Constable Jones on Oldham Road, who hailed a cab and made his way to the scene. Dr Quick had been summoned by neighbours, but Matilda died before the police officer arrived. On being advised that Donohue remained upstairs, Constable Jones, unarmed and alone, made his way to the bedroom, to arrest the murderer. He found Donohue lay on the bed with the knife thrust deep into his stomach. Jones removed it and called for a litter from Kirby Street police station. The wounded man was taken to Ancoats Hospital, where he was treated by the house surgeons, Doctors Hunter and Winter. Donohue was found to have a wound six inches deep, which was dressed before he was placed in the Jardine Ward, guarded by a police officer.

His survival was in doubt from the start and during that night he became delirious, crying out 'Poor Tilda' and 'Come home Tilda.' He died on 13 May, and although he had managed to speak with his doctors and police officers, he did not discuss the crime. The inquests on both assailant and victim were held jointly the following day at the coroner's court before Mr Sidney Smelt, the deputy coroner.

The first witness was Ann Crabtree, the victim's mother, who told the court that her daughter had left home on the last occasion because she was afraid, after Donohue had threatened her and had said to her that he had 'something upstairs which would do for you.' Furthermore, Matilda had told the witness that she had seen a knife under the bed. However, when he had called to ask his wife to return home

Ancoats Hospital, to which Thomas Donohue was taken for treatment after the stabbings. Manchester Faces and Places

with him he had seemed very friendly and had promised to stop being violent towards her.

Sarah Ellen followed her mother in giving evidence and advised the court of the events that followed her sister's decision to return home with her husband. Constable Jones described what had occurred after his arrival at the scene, particularly how he had found Donohue on the bed with the knife protruding from his body just below the ribs, after having first opened his waistcoat and lifted his shirt before stabbing himself.

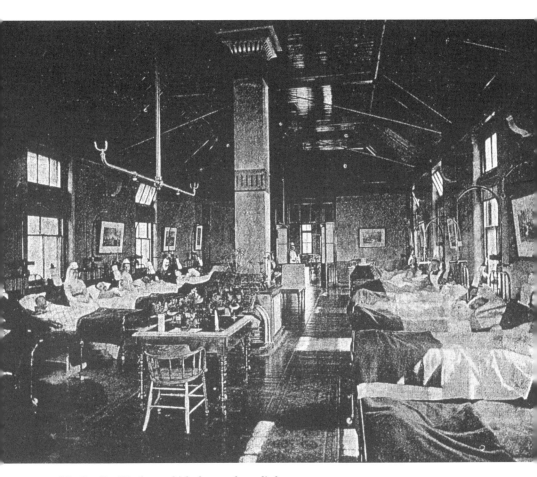

The Jardine Ward, on which the murderer died. Manchester Faces and Places

Evidence was then given by the doctors responsible for the post-mortems. William J Heslop, a police surgeon of Stretford Road, performed one on Matilda. He had found a bruise to the right eye, three small bruises on the right side of her forehead and cuts to her head. The index, middle and ring fingers of her right hand, together with the palm of her left hand had been cut. Between the seventh and eighth ribs there was an incised wound, which passed through the base of the right lung, cut the spinal column and major blood vessels before entering the left lung. The knife had been partially withdrawn and thrust in again, in a downwards direction, entering the liver. Her skull was fractured and the inner layer depressed. Death was caused by internal haemorrhage caused by the wound between the ribs, and would have been almost instantaneous. The cuts to the hands were due to her attempts to defend herself, and the head injuries were the result of falling downstairs.

The following witness Dr J T Winter, medical officer at Ancoats Hospital, told of Donohue's admission at three thirty in the afternoon of 11 May in a state of extreme collapse. He had a puncture wound in the upper part of the abdomen, which despite treatment led to his death at seven forty in the evening of 13 May. The cause of death was shock to the system stemming from the abdomen wound, which passed upwards and backwards in to the left lung. Although he had not admitted any crime, Donohue told Dr Winter at a time when conscious that he had been treated falsely by his wife, and he had been jealous of her former lover.

The proceedings seemed to be drawing to a straightforward conclusion as the murderer's son Denis began his evidence, but there was to be a dramatic revelation that left those in the courtroom stunned. He stated that eighteen years earlier in 1868, his father stabbed his first wife, the witness's mother, to death. Initially, he had been charged with her murder but he was convicted of manslaughter. It is unclear as to whether the authorities had been aware of this, but no indication of this earlier crime had been given by the police at the current inquest, and nor had the press realised what had occurred in the past. It is not known whether Matilda and her family were aware of his history, but again no indication of this was given in their evidence.

Mr Smelt addressed the jury and asked if they had sufficient evidence to enable them to reach a verdict. They indicated that they had, and he asked if they were prepared to find a verdict of wilful murder against Thomas Donohue in the case of Matilda, and suicide in his own case. Without moving from their seats and with a minimum of discussion the jury unanimously called out 'Yes,' and the verdicts were formally recorded.

Having traced details of the first case in 1868 it is surprising how many similarities there are in both crimes.

In May 1868 Thomas Donohue, then employed as a labourer, was living with his wife Mary Ann in Wood Street, Salford. It was not a happy marriage, and he was renowned throughout the district for regularly beating his wife and children. Matters had deteriorated even further during the previous two years as Mary Ann turned more and more to alcohol, and she was often seen in a drunken state. In April 1868 she left her husband and children, but returned five weeks later on 18 May, and the following night the whole street could hear them arguing.

At seven o'clock in the morning of 20 May, he left home to go to work, but after a short time he made his way back to Wood Street. There he met a neighbour, Mrs Johnson, who had helped him care for the children after his wife had left him. He also met two other neighbours and insisted on taking them all to the nearby spirits vaults owned by Mr McGee, which despite the early hour had opened for business. Donohue bought drinks for everyone and told them how miserable he was in the marriage, and now as a result of his having to take time off work to care for the children in her absence, he had lost his job. Furthermore, he complained that she had turned his children against him, and he was now determined to 'end it all.' He finished his glass, stood up and told his neighbours that he had had eleven drinks that morning.

Mrs Johnson followed him out a few minutes later, and as she passed the Donohue home she heard Mary Ann's voice shouting 'Oh Tom, don't. Oh good God, what is this all for?' Shortly afterwards, Donohue came out of the house into the street. Pulling up his flannel singlet he revealed blood streaming from his side, and shouted 'This life is lost through an evil woman.' Mrs Johnson asked him who had done it, and he held up his own arm saying 'This hand has done it.' He urged Mrs Johnson to bring a policeman as he went back into the house.

Constable Barrington arrived at the house to find Donohue in a chair covered in blood from his own wound. Upstairs the officer found Mary Ann dead, lying face down in her nightdress, with a pool of blood to her left side. He arranged for Donohue to be taken to the Dispensary, and called for Dr A W Stork, who pronounced the victim dead. The knife used in the crime lay on the floor close to the body.

The post-mortem on Mary Ann was carried out by Dr Stork, who at the inquest, held at the *White Lion* public house on Wood Street, Salford, stated that he had found four stab wounds to her left side. The most serious was the upper one which had penetrated between the third and fourth ribs and pierced the aorta. Of the other wounds two could have caused death, but one had not been so serious.

Donohue was found to have seven self inflicted wounds, and for a while his life had been in danger. He was placed in the Dispensary where he lapsed into what was described as a state of mental frenzy. This led to his having to be restrained in a strait jacket to prevent him from tearing off his dressings. It was to be twenty-six days before he could be charged, and this was done on 15 June by Superintendent Williams. In reply, Donohue said 'I remember going out to my work that morning, but through my wife I had to go back again, and I lost my work. I got some drink and I don't remember anything after. But since I have been at the Dispensary, from what I have heard, I believe I was the cause of her death.' The following day he was committed to the assizes for trial.

That he had stabbed Mary Ann to death was not in question, but at the trial, his counsel, Mr Pope urged the jury to find his client guilty of the lesser charge of manslaughter. He highlighted the despair his client must have felt as his wife's dependence on alcohol worsened. He called a neighbour, Esther Cotterell who confirmed that she had only ever seen the defendant drunk on one occasion during the past four years. Thus his crime was described as arising from his misery as the marriage deteriorated, and that morning his anger had been fuelled by whisky, which he was not used to drinking, and it was against this backdrop that he killed his wife.

The judge gave what can only be described as a surprisingly sympathetic summing up as far as Donohue was concerned, and it tells us much of the status and expectations of women in mid-Victorian England. The judge pointed to the condition to which the prisoner and his children had been reduced by the deceased's drinking. Furthermore, he suggested that 'Nothing could be more touching than the spectacle of that deserted home – the wife gone away, leaving her children to be cared for she knew not how.'

He continued by stating that 'It was little wonder that the prisoner was a shattered and wrecked man, and it was no wonder that his whole moral being had been shaken, and that such disastrous consequences had followed.' The judge told the jury that if they felt that Donohue had been provoked, the charge could be reduced to manslaughter. As was to occur eighteen years later, after just a few moments of deliberation and without leaving their seats, the jury reached their verdict. He was found guilty of manslaughter and then sentenced to ten years penal servitude.

Thomas Donohue was undoubtedly a vicious and brutal man, prepared to kill a woman for what he perceived as behaviour that wronged him. The first jury seemed prepared to accept that he was a wronged man, provoked into behaving as he did by Mary Ann's behaviour, and that whilst under the influence of alcohol he acted out of character. However, that could not be said of the second crime, as he displayed premeditation and great callousness in lulling Matilda into a false sense of security before brutally killing her. If he had survived his second suicide bid it is unlikely he would have escaped the noose on that occasion.

CHAPTER 8

The Murder of Warder Webb
1888

S hortly after six o'clock on the evening of Thursday, 29 March 1888, Constable Crowther of the Eccles police received information that a suspicious looking individual had been asking for the whereabouts of the home of Salvation Army Captain Alfred Poynter. Within the hour, Crowther had concealed himself in the kitchen of the captain's house. It was not long before he heard someone climbing over the garden wall, and enter through the kitchen window. The intruder crept over to the mantelpiece, where he examined some items. Crowther pounced, secured the offender and upon searching him found two jemmies wrapped in an Oldham newspaper.

The police officer had responded quickly and professionally upon receiving the initial tip off, as he had recognised the arrival in town of twenty-eight-year-old John Jackson, real name Charles Wood Firth, an offender whose speciality was to burglarise the homes of Salvation Army officers. His description and *modus operandi* had been published the the *Police Gazette* and *War Cry*. As Constable Crowther led the subdued Jackson to the police station neither man could have realised the train of events that had been set in motion that would lead to the gallows, less than five months later. Jackson was brought to the county court where Inspector Kelly of the Eccles force, produced a copy of the the *Police Gazette,* giving a description of the prisoner, and also confirming that he was wanted in Bradford, Hull and Oldham. The bench described him as 'an important capture,' before sending him to the Salford Quarter Sessions for sentence. At the sessions he gave his occupation as painter, and he was not represented. The prosecutor, Mr Fletcher, gave details of his criminal background. Jackson was a notorious criminal, who earlier in his career had been imprisoned for six months for horse stealing whilst serving in the army. He had been sent to Wakefield prison from which he escaped on 9 August 1883. However, he was recaptured, and served the remainder of that sentence at Armley prison, Leeds, from which he was released in 1885. Neither rehabilitated nor deterred, his offending continued and for the Eccles burglary he was sentenced to six months imprisonment.

Jackson was sent to Strangeways prison in Manchester, where he seems to have settled into the prison regime without causing any problems. That was until the afternoon of Tuesday, 22 May 1888, when he was asked by prison staff, who assumed he had some knowledge of plumbing and gas fitting, to attend the quarters of Miss Little, the prison matron, as she had reported smelling gas in an upstairs room.

He was escorted to the room by just one staff member, Warder Ralph Webb. It was not long before Miss Little's suspicions were aroused. She was sat in her parlour, immediately below the room in which the two men were supposedly working. She heard a noise and went upstairs, where she found the door to the room was locked from the inside. She called out and a voice replied 'All right,' but as no attempt was made to unlock the door, she ran downstairs and into the main prison to raise the alarm. Some of Webb's colleagues made their way to the room, where the leak was supposedly being repaired. Webb was found mortally wounded with severe head injuries, which had been caused by a blunt instrument. There was no sign of Jackson, but a hole in the ceiling pointed to his escape route. He had gained access to the roof and lowered himself into Southall Street, along which he made his escape.

As he was doing so, Webb was taken to the prison hospital, where he died two hours later. It was discovered that nine shillings and six pence had been stolen from Webb's pockets, and his boots had also been taken. A massive manhunt began immediately, but Jackson had left the vicinity and evaded his pursuers. The hunt for Jackson gripped the country, and was avidly followed in the press. On his first night of freedom, he broke into two houses in Oldham, including of course, that of

MURDER OF A WARDER AT STRANGEWAYS GAOL.

THE MURDER IN THE MATRONS' BED ROOM

The Illustrated Police News

the local Salvation Army Captain. He stole clothes, porter, money and cigars, leaving behind an empty bottle of the drink and the remains of a cigar he had smoked. The burglaries were obviously the work of Jackson, as he also left one of his prison socks behind in one of the houses.

As they had no immediate success in recapturing Jackson, the police issued a wanted notice on 31 May, which not only

Jackson makes his escape over the prison wall. The Illustrated Police News

included a physical description but also a list of his known aliases, which were: Charles Williamson Firth, Charles Wood, Charles William Firth, Charles Wilson, Charles Kitson, John Jackson, Edward Graham, Fred Smith etc. He was described as being 5ft 5in, with a round face, fresh complexion, hazel eyes and dark brown hair. The following physical peculiarities were listed, and these would later prove crucial in his capture: a cut mark on his nose, a scar on the left side of his neck, a mole on his back, and an abscess mark on his groin. He also had a small lump on the first finger of his left hand, and a habit of not looking straight at the person with whom he was in conversation.

As the hue and cry continued, the inquest on forty-five-year-old Ralph Webb was held on Friday, 25 May 1888. Major Preston, the prison governor confirmed that on his arrival at Strangeways the warrant was accompanied by a certificate from the police saying that he had no previous convictions. The prison therefore had no knowledge of his criminal history or his past escape from Wakefield gaol. It had not therefore been thought necessary to make any special arrangements. Ironically, at the exact time the murder took place a colleague

The prison wall that faces onto Southall Street as it is today. The author

was on his way to relieve Webb, who was due to have a tea break.

Webb was buried a few days later at Salford Cemetery, and the funeral procession comprised three mourning coaches and the hearse, which left his home on Cotham Street, Strangeways, and made its way along Chapel Street, Oldfield Road, Regent Road and Eccles New Road, where the cemetery was located. In the hearse, Webb's uniform, cap and belt lay amongst the many floral tributes on the coffin lid. Escorted by fellow warders dressed in full uniform with crepe armbands, the crowds lining the route expressed their sympathies for the widow and her six-year-old daughter.

On arrival at the mortuary chapel, Reverend Edwin Walker, Minister of Pendleton Congregational Chapel read the service. Also present were Reverend Dreaper, the Prison Chaplain, together with the Governor, Major Preston and Miss Little, the Matron. Later at the graveside, Mrs Webb became so distressed that she had to be helped away. Afterwords, Reverend Edward

The home of the murdered prison officer and his family. The Illustrated Police News

Reeve, Rector of St Alban's Cheetwood initiated a public appeal for the widow and daughter.

Meanwhile, the search for Jackson continued. Although he might have made tracks for anywhere in the country, it was thought that he had remained in the Manchester area, or more likely gone to his native Yorkshire. The police kept watch at race meetings, and there were many supposed sightings: for instance someone reported seeing him drinking in an Oldham pub on the night of the escape: police were called to the *Golden Quoits Inn* at Greengate, Salford, where Jackson was said to be drinking: he was also reported to be begging in Ordsall, another district of Salford. However, these all proved to be false leads.

Jackson was eventually captured on Friday, 15 June 1888, but had been held in police custody for several hours before his true identity was discovered, whereupon he told the police of events since the crime. Having reached the roof of the matron's house, he lowered himself onto the roof of a lower building, from which he easily reached the prison's perimeter wall. He spotted two boys and asked if anyone was about: on being told there was nobody in the area, he dropped ten feet to the street and made for Red Bank, a densely populated district, frequented by criminals. He insisted that he had not known of Webb's death until the following day, and shortly after his escape he borrowed a coat from a friendly pub landlord having stolen the hat of a young boy, who was later found crying in the street. He made his way to Oldham, and was seen by two young girls who informed the police. In Oldham, he committed the reported burglaries, and later travelled to Halifax, where he shaved off his moustache. He then moved between Leeds and Halifax, before deciding to stay in Bradford. He survived by stealing, and admitted a burglary in Horton, and by borrowing from friends in Halifax: however, as he was well known in that town, he decided upon Bradford, where he was not known. He used the name Thomas Harrison and spent much of his time drinking in local public houses. His resemblance to the fugitive was commented on, as many wanted posters had been circulated throughout the north of England, but he managed to allay suspicion by responding in a jocular manner.

He lodged with a man named Booth, but moved after just a few days. At one o'clock in the morning of Monday, 11 June Booth was awakened by a noise, and upon looking out of his bedroom window he saw a man attempting to break into his house. Booth shouted out and the would-be burglar ran off and disappeared into the yard in a nearby inn. Booth rushed out and realising where the other man was, dragged him out of a privy, to find his recently departed lodger. There was a fierce struggle during which Jackson suffered a severe cut to his head, which stunned him.

Police Constable Flood was passing and upon hearing the disturbance, went to the scene, arrested the burglar and escorted him to the police office, where he was held overnight, his true identity still not known. He gave his name as Thomas Harrison, a joiner of Garnett Street, Bradford. He was searched and found to have a small amount of loose change and a knife in his possession.

At 9.30 the following morning, Detective Talbot made his routine daily inspection of the overnight arrests. Talbot's suspicions were immediately aroused by the prisoner Harrison, who so closely matched the description of the Strangeway's fugitive. He noticed a distinct mark on the prisoner's finger, and he asked him to remove some of his clothing. There were more physical similarities, namely a scar on his groin, a scar on his neck and a mole on his back.

Talbot challenged the prisoner who replied 'It's time it was finished. I am Jackson, the man you want.' To confirm the prisoner's identity, Talbot visited Birstall and brought Jackson's two brothers, Alfred and Harry who identified him.

He appeared in chains before local magistrates on Tuesday, 12 June, his subdued demeanour reflecting his desperate situation. Chief Constable Withers advised the court of the previous day's events, and the offences committed by the prisoner in Bradford, but that he was wanted on far more serious matters by the Manchester Police, who had two officers present in court. One of them, Detective Sergeant George Graham, identified the prisoner as Jackson. Throughout the hearing, as Detective Graham sought for the prisoner to be sent back to Manchester,

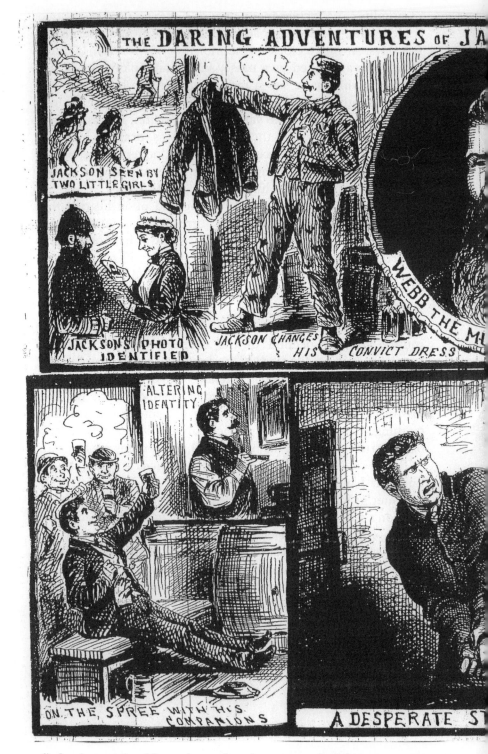

Jackson's escapades whilst on the run, kept the country enthralled. The Illustrated Police News

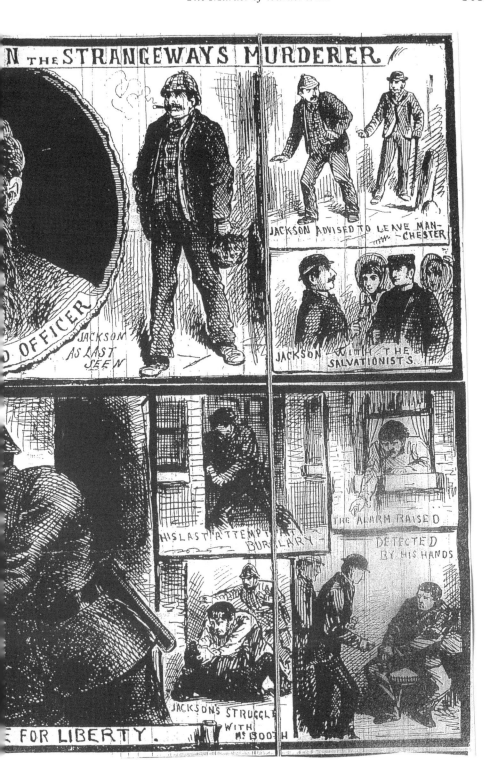

DETECTIVE TALBOT

JACKSON FULLY COMMITTED

The astute Detective Talbot was responsible for putting Jackson in the dock for murder. The Illustrated Police News

Jackson rested his arms on the dock and lay his head on them, never looking up. He was taken to Manchester, and on the following day appeared at the Manchester police court, where he was committed for trial at the next Manchester Assizes.

As he awaited his trial, stories of what occurred whilst he was on the run began to emerge. He was a personable man, and a renowned amateur vocalist. Whilst evading capture, he supposedly spent a good deal of time in Bradford's *White Bear Inn,* singing his favourite songs such as *The Thorn* and *The Pilgrim of Love,* whilst behind him was a poster giving details of Webb's murder and Jackson's description. He was also said to have displayed great nerve whilst stood in the taproom, as a man, in the nearby parlour said he knew the fugitive and could identify him. He was said to have broken into a house in Beech Grove, Bradford, where he slept in the absent householder's bed overnight, and upon leaving he waved a cheery farewell to neighbours. In another house he broke into, he dined on a meal of cold mutton and salad before washing his hair. There is obviously more than a hint of the apocryphal in these stories, but they contributed to his mystique and what the press called the 'almost unheard of coolness of the man.'

The trial took place on Friday, 13 July 1888, and was attended by a large number of spectators, including a group of ladies, who found seats close to the prisoner in the dock, from whom he tried to shield his face throughout the proceedings. He certainly did not cut the dashing figure many were no doubt expecting, as he seemed aware of his fate from the beginning, and he looked sad and solitary.

The prosecutor, Mr Addison, gave the details of the case: the dying warder found in the matron's room: the hole in the ceiling: the missing prisoner: and the alleged confession made

The murderer as he appeared in court during his trial. The Illustrated Police News

PORTRAIT OF JACKSON SKETCHED IN COURT.

to the police in Bradford after his capture. As the evidence mounted Jackson seemed to visibly shrink in the dock: he rarely raised his eyes, other than when apparently trying to read the judge's expressions.

One particularly dramatic moment during the prosecution evidence, was the appearance of the victim's widow, Mrs Webb, who was called to confirm that the knife found in Jackson's possession in Bradford had belonged to her late husband.

The defence was led by Mr Wharton who put forward the theory that the injuries to Webb had been caused accidentally as he stood up suddenly having knelt down to smell for gas: as he did so he banged his head against a hammer that Jackson was holding in his hand. As this ingenious theory continued, Jackson looked over towards the jury, more in hope than expectation.

Indeed, Mr Wharton appears to have been fully aware of the weakness of his case, and in a last desperate act, he drew the jury's attention to the presence of the accused's father John Firth who was in court. Wharton implored the jury to spare him the grief of having his son meet his end at the hands of the executioner. Father and son were sat facing each other in court and both became visibly distressed. The older man, a respectable plumber by trade, elicited much sympathy, but it was obvious that Wharton's emotional appeal had nothing to do with the facts of the case. It was then time or the judge's summing up, but before he started, Mr Firth rose from his seat and left the courtroom, unable to face the ordeal any further. Mr Justice Grantham immediately disposed of the defence argument that the death was accidental, describing it as 'a monstrous improbability.' Throughout the summing up, Jackson became visibly more dejected. He was led down to the cells as the jury retired, but he did not have long to wait. After just seven minutes, the jury returned with the inevitable guilty verdict, whereupon Jackson slumped forward in the dock, covering his face with a handkerchief.

Asked by the clerk if he had anything to say before sentence was passed, he responded in a scarcely audible voice that he had not intended to kill Webb. The judge then sentenced him to death.

The execution was scheduled for 8 am on Tuesday, 7 August 1888, and by 7.30 am a crowd of one thousand had gathered outside of Strangeways Prison gates. As 8 am approached the crowd became silent, until this was broken by the sound of the town hall clock striking the hour, which was quickly followed by the shrill clanging of the prison bell confirming that the execution had been carried out. This was followed by the raising of a black flag on the prison flag pole.

Following the abolition of public hangings in 1868, it was still common practice to allow journalists to attend prison hangings, and three were present at Jackson's execution. Their accounts, together with those provided by prison officials meant that details of the condemned individual's final hours became known.

He had gone to bed at 8 o'clock the previous night but slept little, and spent a restless night. He breakfasted on bread and butter at 6 am, and was attended by Reverend Dreaper, who later described the condemned man as being 'undoubtedly and most sincerely penitent.' The chaplain also later confirmed that Jackson had admitted to him that he had deliberately hit Webb on the side of the head as he stood up and had turned his gaze away from Jackson.

At 7.57 am the executioner, James Berry, entered the condemned cell, and shook hands with the prisoner, who was by now pale and subdued: he was pinioned and led the ten paces from the cell to the scaffold: he was placed on the drop, his footstraps were adjusted: Jackson's lips were seen to be moving but he uttered no sound: a white cap was placed over his head and as Reverend Dreaper said 'Have mercy upon this man's soul' the drop opened.

The suspended body twitched slightly for a moment, and the prison doctors then examined the pulse and heart, and found a small trickle of blood coming from the nose: death was said to have been instantaneous, and Berry was happy with the result of his work, having calculated a drop of 5′6″ for the 10 stones 7lbs prisoner. In line with tradition, the body was left hanging for one hour, before being cut down for the post-mortem to be immediately carried out, at which death was deemed to have been due to a 'fracture to the neck caused by hanging.'

Jackson's father, John Firth of Hudders Road, Birstall, petitioned the Home Secretary, prior to the execution to have his son's remains returned to him for burial, but this was refused, which meant that Jackson was executed and buried on the same site as the murder he had committed.

CHAPTER 9

The Moston Axe Murder
1888

Unrequited love provided the motive for a particularly brutal murder, that occurred in Moston at about noon on Thursday, 1 March 1888. The victim was forty-two-year-old Mary Miller, who, although a married woman, had been separated from her husband for nine years. Mary lived at 6 St Mary's Road, Moston, with Isabella, her twenty-one-year-old daughter. Isabella was a single woman, who had recently given birth to a baby, and as a result, had had to give up her job in Manchester, and had returned to live with her mother.

Mary took in lodgers, and two young women, who worked at a nearby factory, were also living there. She supplemented her income by dressmaking, at which she was helped by Isabella. It is clear, from the statements made by their neighbours at the time, that mother and daughter were popular and well respected in the district, where people do not seem to have been particularly concerned that Isabella was a single mother.

Also living in the house was Alfred Gell, a thirty-two-year-old wheelwright. He had been staying there since mid-January 1888, and in all of that time he had been unemployed. He had paid no rent to Mrs Miller, which was a source of great annoyance to Isabella, who thought that he was taking advantage of her mother's good nature.

The nature of the relationship between Mary and Gell was unclear at the time, but it was the most significant contributory factor to the crime. They had known each other for some time prior to his coming to stay in January, and Isabella believed that their relationship was not intimate, but at his trial for Mary's murder, the prosecution described them as seeming to live as man and wife. A neighbour, Benjamin

Royston, who knew them both, believed that Gell loved her, but this was not reciprocated by Mary, who viewed him simply as a friend. There is no record of Gell claiming that their relationship was intimate, before, during or after the trial. Whatever the nature of their relationship was, or had been, it is obvious that his feelings were not returned by the end of February by Mary, who wanted rid of him.

Mary and Gell often met at the home of Mr Royston and his wife, so that Isabella would not be upset by seeing them together. Gell was also in the habit of calling to see Royston on his own to speak with him, and he did so on the evening of 28 February, at about 8.30 pm. Gell confessed to Royston, that he had sensed a growing distance between himself and Mary, and as a result he had deliberately started scurrilous rumours about her, the precise details of which were never revealed. These had been heard by a friend of Mary's, who had told her of them.

Gell now bitterly regretted having done so, as he realised it would undoubtedly turn Mary against him even more. He asked if Royston would speak a good word for him to Mary, and went on to say, 'I love Mrs Miller. I am fond of Mrs Miller. I intend to have Mrs Miller, and I will finish her first, before anyone else shall have her.' At the time of the visit, his friend was later to confirm that Gell had been sober.

Gell again called on Royston on the following evening of 29 February, at 8 pm. He told his neighbour that he had seen Mary earlier in the day, and she had indicated that she wanted to talk with him, and asked him to await her at the Royston home. Gell lay down and slept for some time, before Mary eventually arrived.

As she entered the room, Gell immediately stood up and greeted her by saying 'Good evening.' However, Mary snapped 'Shut up' and continued by telling him she wanted nothing more to do with him. Gell approached her in a friendly manner as though trying to calm her, but she would have nothing to do with him and pulled away. He attempted to kiss her, but she shoved him away, shouting 'Alfred Gell, I hate you, I hate you.' She then turned towards her neighbour and said to him 'Now Mr Royston, I will tell you something about him, and you will never speak to him any more, after I have told you what he said about me.'

Gell suggested to Mary that they go home, but she replied, as though sensing at that moment that she had placed herself in a dangerous situation, by saying 'I will stop where I can have protection. Mr Royston will protect me.' At this, Gell became extremely angry, and grabbed her by the neck. He dragged her out of the house, and as they reached the gate, Royston, who had followed them outside, managed to loosen Gell's grip on Mary, who returned inside her neighbour's house, with her hair hanging down and her bonnet having been knocked off her head. Mrs Royston helped her straighten her hair, and to put her bonnet on, after which Mary went home by the back door.

However, Gell caught her up and they entered Mary's house together, where they were greeted by one of the lodgers, Elizabeth Neville, who later testified that she had noticed nothing wrong. Mary went to her room upstairs, and Gell lay down on the sofa, where he normally slept, and where he must have spent a restless night going over recent events again and again.

The next morning, Elizabeth Neville rose at 5 am, as she had an early start at the factory. She saw Gell being sick, before she left the house alone, as her friend, who also lodged at the house, was away. Isabella came downstairs shortly afterwards to light the fire. She also saw Gell being sick, but she had little sympathy for him. He told her that he had found work and was going to leave the house for good. She replied that she was very pleased as it meant she would not have to see him again. Gell left at 7 am, apparently for good. However, that was not to be so, for he was to return just a few hours later.

At a few minutes before noon, William Clysedale was in his shop, situated opposite the Miller household, together with John Morley, an egg and butter merchant from Salford. As they discussed business, they saw Isabella appear at her front door, her head and face covered in blood. They heard her cry out 'Will no one come in: he has come in and is killing my mother.'

The two men rushed across the road and ran into the house, and as they did so Clysedale saw the back of Gell rushing out of the back door. Police Constable Richard Robinson was nearby, keeping an eye on a suspicious looking beggar, when he was told of the incident. At almost the same moment, he saw a man running away from the direction of the house, across a field towards Moston cemetery. Putting two and two together, and suspecting a link, he gave chase and pursued Gell for about a quarter of a mile. Eventually, Gell stopped, and turned to face the officer, saying 'Put the handcuffs on me.'

Constable Robinson asked Gell what he had done, to which his prisoner replied 'I don't know.' Nevertheless, Gell was taken to the local police station, where later in the day, he

The dramatic events which occurred in the few minutes between Alfred Gell murdering Mary Miller, and his capture after a brief chase. The Illustrated Police News

would be charged with the murder of Mary, blood stains having been found on the sleeve of his jacket.

Whilst the police officer was chasing Gell, Clysedale and Morley had found a scene of carnage in Mary's home. Isabella had suffered serious head injuries, but when they went into the back yard, they found Mary with extensive wounds to her head. They carried her into the house, where they put her in a chair, attempting to make her as comfortable as they could. Whilst they awaited medical assistance, the two men found an axe covered in blood, and a man's hat on the ground.

Mr W J Pegg, surgeon, of 770 Oldham Road, Newton Heath was quickly at the scene of the tragedy. He found Mary alive but unconscious, and he noticed a large wound on the left side of her head: there were also a number of other wounds towards the back of the head. She was obviously close to death, and Dr Pegg therefore left her, and went next door, where Isabella had been taken, as she seemed to have a better chance of recovery than her mother, and indeed, Mary died just a few minutes later.

Isabella was taken to the Royal Infirmary, where a deposition was taken from her later that evening, in the presence of Mr J H P Leresche, the stipendiary magistrate, Mr R A Armitage, a justice of the peace, and also present was Gell. Isabella's deposition gave some indication of what had occurred just a few hours earlier.

She gave details of the events of the previous months, and how that morning, Gell had promised to leave for good. She then focused on events from about noon, when he had returned to the house unexpectedly. When Isabella had asked why, he had replied 'I have got some work.' Mary came out from the scullery, which opened into the room where the other two were talking. Isabella replied 'It's a good job, you can go now.' Mary returned into the scullery, as Isabella tended to the baby, who was lying on the sofa in front of her.

Suddenly, Isabella felt a violent blow to the back of her head, which stunned her for a moment. However, she was able to rise, and as she made for the front door, she felt herself struck on the head once more, but she could not remember how many blows in all were struck. She reached the front door, where she shouted for help, before passing out. When she regained consciousness she was being cared for by a neighbour, Mrs Hulse, and Dr Pegg then arrived.

Isabella continued by stating that Gell did not like her, as she had often expressed concern to her mother about his staying in the house. Gell had quarrelled with Isabella regularly, and she insisted that he had hit her with his fists on one previous occasion.

When asked if he had anything to say, the prisoner denied having hit Isabella in the past, but acknowledged that they had quarrelled regularly, but she had threatened him with a poker. She strenuously denied this accusation, and she added that not only had he hit her, he had also threatened to break her back.

Gell was then taken back to Old Trafford police station, and next morning he made his first appearance before the magistrates, at the county police court at Strangeways. After hearing from Constable Robinson and Mr Clysedale, the bench remanded the prisoner in custody for another week.

The inquest on Mary opened on Saturday, 3 March, at the *Railway Hotel,* Newton Heath, before Mr P Price, the district coroner, and the first business of the day was for the jury to visit Mary's home, where they viewed her body. Formal identification was made by Edward Miller, a general agent of 65 Duke Street, Old Trafford. He was the estranged husband of the dead woman, as they had separated almost ten years earlier, and he had not seen her for five years. He had identified the body but knew nothing of the circumstances surrounding her death.

Dr Pegg had performed a post-mortem, the results of which he gave to the jury, and they confirmed the savagery of the attack upon her. There were seven wounds to her head, the largest of which was on the left side, which led down to a compound fracture of the skull, in which there was a large hole, out of which a piece of bone had been displaced. This, and the other six wounds had caused massive injuries to the skull and brain. There were no other wounds to the body, and no disease in any other organs.

Death had resulted from extensive fractures of the skull and shock. It had required a great deal of force to inflict the injuries to the head, and Mary had been subjected to a prolonged, deliberate and vicious assault from behind, with an axe: this was certainly no accident. It was believed that Mary had heard the assault being committed on her daughter, and had run out of the scullery to see what was happening. She herself was then attacked in the backyard into which she had run, in an attempt to escape. After this, Gell is alleged to have dropped the axe and also to have lost his hat during the attack, and then run across the nearby field, before being caught by Constable Robinson.

It was not possible to conclude the inquest, as Isabella was not well enough to leave the Royal Infirmary to attend the hearing. It was adjourned until 14 March to enable her to do so. Permission had been granted for Mary's funeral to proceed, and it had been planned to hold it that afternoon at 4 pm at Harpurhey cemetery. However, her family decided to take her body to Derbyshire for burial at Hope, near Castleton. Her coffin was to be taken by train from Manchester at 6 pm that evening.

Mary's body had remained in her house in the days since the crime took place, and its removal on Saturday afternoon was the occasion of an extraordinary demonstration of loyalty to her memory by her neighbours. A hearse came to collect her body, and the large crowd that had assembled outside kept a respectful silence as her coffin was placed in the hearse before being taken to the railway station.

However, it was known that her estranged husband, had made some disparaging remarks about her morals, which had incensed her friends and neighbours. There had been a police presence in the house since the crime was committed, but they were about to leave and hand over possession to her husband, who was in the house. Those in the crowd, who were now at the back and front of the house were shouting abuse at him and vowing to 'Do for him' if they could get hold of him. The police advised him that it would be unsafe to stay there on his own, and it was decided that he should leave as quickly as possible. He appeared at the front door, surrounded by seven police officers, to be met by a loud chorus of booing and hissing. Still surrounded by his bodyguards, he walked to

Oldham Road, followed by the angry and vociferous crowd. A cab had been summoned, and on reaching Oldham Road, he leapt into it, and as he was driven off, he could still no doubt hear the crowd for some time.

Meanwhile, Isabella remained in a critical condition in the Royal Infirmary, which led to the hearings due before the coroner and the magistrates to be postponed. However, Gell was produced at the magistrates court on 9 March, and although the proceedings were cancelled, he asked to speak to Sergeant Moses Thompson, to whom he indicated that he wished to make a statement. The sergeant took his statement down whilst the prisoner was in the dock, and this was to prove to be extremely controversial at his eventual trial.

Isabella was able to attend the inquest hearing of 28 March, despite still suffering from her injuries, which necessitated her appearing with her head bound in cotton wool, which was covered by a black velvet hood. Having listened to her evidence about the events of 1 March, the jury immediately returned a verdict that Mary had been wilfully murdered by Gell.

The following day, Isabella attended the adjourned hearing before the magistrates, and at this hearing the prosecution sought his committal to the assizes on the additional charge of attempting to murder Isabella. She was again able to give evidence, but on being shown the axe used in the attacks against her and her mother she turned deathly pale and it seemed that she might faint. However, she was given a glass of water and recovered her composure. She identified the axe and confirmed it was usually kept in the scullery.

Formal committal was postponed until 5 April, as they needed to hear the medical evidence, which was provided by Mr E T Milner, resident surgical officer at the Royal Infirmary. Isabella had suffered four severe head wounds, three of which were on the crown, and the other was to the right side of her head. The latter was only a crack, but the others had been much more dangerous, and had caused extensive injuries. Considerable force had been used, and the axe produced in court was the likely cause. Having heard this evidence, and that of Constable Robinson, about the chase, for which the jury congratulated him, Gell was committed to the assizes for trial. However, before this took place, some details of Sergeant Thompson's discussion with the prisoner at the hearing on 9 March, were given, but at this stage it was only the information that related to Isabella's case.

Sergeant Thompson confirmed to the court that Gell had said that he wanted to make a statement, and part of it was read to the magistrates, and it read: 'If it had not been for 'Bell, we should have lived happily together: she was always calling me names. I went away to Newton Heath, and when I returned home, I entered the back door. Mrs Miller saw me take the axe. I struck 'Bell on the head with it, and she screamed. Mrs Miller was washing and came to the inner door, but as she saw 'Bell she ran away.'

Gell's solicitor, Mr Davy made much of the fact that it had not been signed by the prisoner, to which the sergeant responded by stating that he had not asked Gell to do so, as he did not think that he would later deny making it. However, the matter was left until the trial, which began at Manchester Assizes on Friday, 27 April before Mr Justice Charles, and when asked for his plea, Gell replied in a firm voice 'Not guilty.'

The prosecution case was conducted by Mr Foard and Mr McKeand, and they relied heavily on the evidence already presented before the magistrates and the coroner's courts. The evidence provided by Isabella Miller, Benjamin Royston, William Clysedale, Constable Robinson and the medical evidence, combined to present a compelling case against Gell.

Furthermore, the whole of his confession was given by sergeant Thompson, and that part which related to Mary's death read: 'When she saw 'Bell she ran back and was going out of the back door, when I struck her with the axe. She fell with her head on the closet step and did not move, only her eyes. I did it all in a few seconds.'

Gell was represented by Mr Cottingham, who insisted that his client had not made a confession to Sergeant Thompson. As for his client's hat which was found at the scene, as though it had fallen off in a struggle or as he ran away, Mr Cottingham stated that it had in fact been thrown after the prisoner, by

Isabella, when he had left the house at 7 am. This was strenuously denied by the young woman, but the defence had made much of her admitted dislike for Gell, which they implied would lead her to lie about him.

One of the defence's main witnesses was John Morley, who had not been called by the prosecution, despite arriving at the scene with his friend Mr Clysedale. Mr Cottingham attempted to exploit the minor discrepancies between the evidence given by the two men. Also of significance, according to Mr Cottingham, was the reply given by Isabella at the time of the crimes, to Mr Morley's question 'Who has committed this crime?' To which she replied 'Oh a man, a man.' This was seen as hugely important by the defence when viewed alongside her screams at the door, when crying for help, as on that occasion also, she had mentioned no specific name. Surely, it was argued, if she had known the attacker, she would have mentioned him by name.

Constable Robinson was questioned about the suspicious looking beggar he had been watching at that time, and Mr Cottingham implied that the crimes had been carried out by this mystery stranger.

Having considered all of these issues, the jury returned with a guilty verdict after just five minutes, and Gell was sentenced to death. There was to be no serious attempt to gain a reprieve, and as he awaited execution in Strangeways gaol, the governor gave permission for two friends to visit him, and also his father and brothers. However, only one friend visited him, but none of his family, although a brother he had not seen for seven years wrote to him. Whilst held in the prison, his mother had died on 12 March, and although she had some inkling that her son was in some kind of trouble, they did not tell her to what extent. Gell's father, John, was a village constable in Lincolnshire, and would not write to him or visit him, until the trial was over.

The visitor asked the press to keep his identity secret, although it was probably Benjamin Royston who kept in touch with his old friend. His correspondence with the prisoner was published, and in keeping with the wishes of the visitor, any details that might point to his identity were removed. Those written by the prisoner before the trial give some insight into the conditions he was living under, and his growing sense of isolation:

HM Prison, Strangeways, March 28 1888
Mr........., I have just received a letter from a brother that I have not seen for seven years, my poor mother died on the 12 inst. She asked them what great trouble her boy Alf was in, but they never told her, they was advised not, this brother has not seen home of three years he's married and lives near London. They sent him word after she was dead. I never knew she was ill whilst my solicitor mentioned a word or two. So you may guess how this has upset me. I've wondered why you had not been to see me lately. I thought...........would have been coming. I'm so glad for any body to come. I did like them sandwiches they was far better than the dinner, They don't send much in when any body pays for a dinner and I expect they charge a shilling, hunger is a sharp thorn I hope you are well and a bit more trade to do. I was glad you sent me a paper. Somebody sent me 2 big cakes buttered and some corn beef and coffee on the Monday after you came last, my lawyer was going to make some arrangements about getting me some food sent instead to prison diet, but I'm on it yet, I'm not allowed to work, so I have to pass my time reading but days seem so long and dreary, I've never had a chance to speak to my solicitor since a week last Thursday I think he's been in Lincolnshire, but I'll let you know particulars.

Another letter was sent to the same man, a few weeks later, which read:

HM Prison, Strangeways, April 16th 1888
Mr ...., I feel in good spirits today. Just a line to say I'm quite well. Hoping things are going well with you. The Assizes commence on 27th I believe, time seems long to me, you have forgot to send me a paper I suppose as I had been expecting one. I've had no letter from home yet but hears my father has received a quantity of letters since I've been in prison. Being Constable for our village he refuses to answer any letters until my trial is over forward me a E. News any time you can remember poor OLD ALF.

Gell's friend wrote to the prisoner's father after the trial, hoping that some contact could be established, but the following reply was received:

Baumber, May 7 1888
Dear sir, - I am very much obliged to you for your kindness to my unfortunate son. If they allow you to see him tell him I really cannot come to see him. I shall see his looks as long as I live. Just had to bury his poor mother. Now this job is more than I can bear at present. If he has any things in pawn will you oblige by sending them to me. Send me word where I can send a P.O.O. for the money by return. Tell him to prepare to meet his dear mother in Heaven, as I can never write to him any more.

JOHN GELL
Baumber, Horncastle, Lincolnshire

On the eve of his execution, Gell slept quite well and awoke at 7 am. He breakfasted on buttered bread and tea, after which he met with the prison chaplain, the Reverend John Dreaper, who remained with him. At a few minutes before 8 am, the hangman, James Berry, entered the condemned cell and pinioned Gell, who stated 'Isabella Miller, I die an innocent man.' He made his way to the scaffold, in the prison yard, wearing an overcoat to protect him from the cold. As Berry made the final adjustments, whilst he stood on the drop, Gell noticed the members of the press, to whom he said in a loud firm voice, 'Isabella Miller, I hope you have had your revenge. Goodbye. God bless you. I die an innocent man.'

The noose had been placed around his neck, and as the white cap was pulled over his head, he said 'The Lord have mercy on my soul. I am now about to leave this earth forever.' The bolt was drawn, and death was said by the press to have been almost instantaneous, although for a few seconds, there were muscular contractions of the legs, and his knees jerked up and down, which one journalist described as being 'exceedingly unpleasant to witness.'

Although he professed his innocence at the very end, he actually accepted limited responsibility after his trial. Gell's version was given some publicity by the friend who had visited him, but clearly without a great deal of conviction. Gell insisted that Isabella had taunted him, which provoked him into hitting her with his fists, and that Mrs Miller then rushed in with the axe. Mary's fatal injuries were caused in the struggle he had with her to take possession of the axe.

It is unlikely that there would have been a different verdict or sentence if he had presented this version of the crimes at his trial.

CHAPTER 10

A Triumph for Detective Caminada
1889

Victorian Manchester's foremost detective was Chief Inspector Jerome Caminada, and of the many murder cases he investigated, the most famous was that which he described in his memoirs as 'The Mystery Of A Four-Wheeled Cab,' in which he utilised all of his experience and powers of deduction. It began with the discovery of a man close to death, in a cab, in the city centre, on the evening of 26 February 1889, and the police had firstly to determine whether a crime had taken place, and secondly, if so, who had committed it.

At about 6.40 pm that evening, cabman Henry Goulding was at the stand close to Manchester Cathedral when a young man and his older companion approached. The younger of the pair asked to be taken to a notorious public house called the *Three Arrows*. Goulding took them and was asked to wait for them outside of the pub, which was in the city centre. As he waited, Goulding smoked his pipe, until his passengers emerged about twenty minutes later. The older man, who came out first, was walking steadily and got into the cab without having to be helped. He was immediately followed by the younger man, who asked that they be taken to 43 Stretford Road.

Goulding drove along Deansgate, Peter Street and Oxford Road, but as he approached Cambridge Street

Detective Chief Inspector Caminada, Manchester's most famous Victorian police officer, whose skills led to the solving of 'The Manchester Cab Mystery'.
Twenty-five Years of Detective Life (vol II)

he had to slow down to a walking pace as a large crowd had gathered to watch a circus parade, and the roads were blocked. After about one hundred yards, he began to drive more quickly, but as he did so, a passer-by shouted out that the young man had jumped out of the cab, and had run off along Cambridge Street. Goulding looked down and saw that the cab's near side door was open. On looking inside the cab, he found the older man alone on the back seat, with his head down on the front seat. He tried to rouse him, but the man told him to go away, seemingly drunk and insensible. Anxious that he should be paid his fare, Goulding decided to return to the cathedral, in the hope of finding a police officer.

Here, Goulding found Police Constable Jackman, and he explained what had occurred, and he hoped he could be assisted in obtaining the fare that was due to him. The officer found the man in what he also initially thought was a drunken state, and told the cabman to drive to the nearby Albert Street police station. However, during the journey, the constable became very concerned about the man, whose condition appeared to be deteriorating rapidly. He called to Goulding to make for the Royal Infirmary. As they arrived, Constable Jackman and Goulding carried the man towards the entrance, but as they did so, he took one last deep intake of breath and died.

As it was a suspicious death, Detective Caminada was put in charge of the initial enquiry, and even though as yet he had no medical evidence, Caminada was not a man to wait around. During the next few days, he demonstrated just why he had become so well known and respected. In his report of the incident, Constable Jackman noted that the deceased's clothing looked as though it had been interfered with, and there was only a small amount of change on him, when from his appearance he seemed to be a gentleman who would have more cash with him. Also, when Caminada looked at the body, he noticed from marks on the bridge of the nose, that he wore spectacles, and although he had two spectacle cases in his pockets, the spectacles themselves, which Caminada subsequently learnt were gold-rimmed, were nowhere to be found.

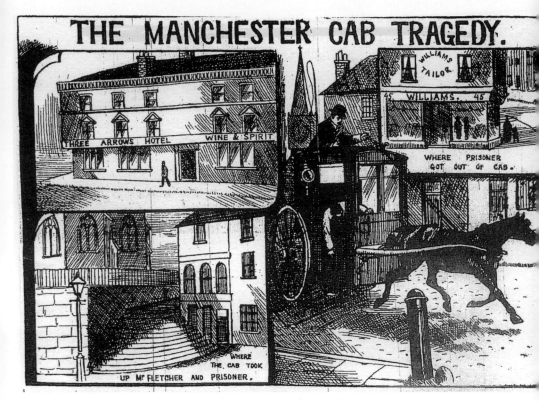

The route of the cab journey that was to lead to death. The Illustrated Police News

Caminada instinctively knew that the still unidentified man had been the victim of foul play, but as yet there was still no evidence that he had been murdered. The first task was to identify the body, and this was done the morning after the incident. A cheque book from the Manchester and Southport Bank was found on him and he was identified through this.

The dead man was fifty-year-old John Fletcher, a paper manufacturer, with business premises in the city, but who had lived in Birkdale, near Southport. He had come to Manchester the previous day to attend the sale of a mill at the *Mitre Hotel*. He left his office in Canon Street at 1 pm, and his nephew, John Robert Fletcher, told Caminada that his uncle had in his possession a wallet containing £5, and a gold watch and chain, and he had also been wearing a pair of gold-rimmed spectacles.

He spent the afternoon in the *Mitre Hotel*, where he was seen by several business associates who knew him well. He left saying he was going to Sinclair's Oyster Rooms, on Deansgate, for something to eat. Caminada followed the trail and found Edward Lait, who had a dried fish and game stall, near to Sinclair's. Lait knew the deceased, and at some time after 6 pm, on the night in question, he had noticed him in conversation with a younger man, whose identity he did not know. The older man appeared to have been drinking. Another paper merchant who knew the deceased and had seen him at Sinclair's, confirmed to Caminada that at this stage he had been wearing his gold watch and chain.

The detective next visited the *Three Arrows,* where the landlady, Mary Elizabeth Frost, confirmed that she had seen two men fitting the descriptions given to her, in her public house on the evening of 26 February at about 7 pm. However, she had not taken much notice of what they had done or said, and could offer no other help. Nevertheless, this limited information had helped the detective establish a sequence of events from the time Mr Fletcher had left the *Mitre Hotel* on his own, and seemingly with all of his possessions, to the time he and the younger man had hired Goulding's cab. He had then traced their movements together to the time that the younger man jumped out of the cab, leaving his companion close to death, with his cash and other valuables missing. Furthermore, he had traced the owner of 43 Stretford Road, which was a lock-up tailor's shop, who did not know anyone fitting the description of the younger man. Clearly, he had tempted his older companion to accompany him there, but how he did so is not known.

Satisfied that there had been a crime of some description committed, Caminada turned his attention to identifying the young man, whom he now suspected of robbery at the very least, and possibly of murder.

The inquest on John Fletcher opened on 1 March before the city's deputy coroner, Sidney Smelt. A post-mortem had been performed by Dr John Barker, house physician at the Royal Infirmary, soon after Fletcher had been pronounced dead. Charles Estcourt, the city analyst, had been sent three sealed jars, one of which was labelled 'Contents of upper part of small intestines – Mr Fletcher's case;' another was labelled 'stomach and contents of Mr Fletcher;' and the third was labelled 'Fluid from the abdominal cavity, removed Friday, March 1st at 2 pm: case of Mr Fletcher.' The analyst had not completed his investigations, and following formal evidence of identification, the inquest was adjourned to allow the police to make further investigations.

However, Caminada was provided with advance notice of the analyst's findings and the post-mortem. On opening the sealed jars containing some of Fletcher's insides, the city analyst had noted a strong smell of alcohol and nothing else. One of the tests he performed was to search for chloroform, which results from the decomposition of chloral hydrate, and he did find a trace. Dr John Barker had assisted Dr Ernest Reynolds to perform a post-mortem, and no external markings which could have contributed to the death were found. Tests to find other poisons had proved negative. Caminada was thus aware that traces of chloral, a colourless liquid used as a sedative, had been found. This prompted the detective's memory, as he remembered reading a routine crime report sent by the Liverpool police of the theft of a quantity of chloral, on Tuesday, 19 February, from a chemist's shop. The description of the thief matched that of the younger man in his current case. Caminada interviewed the chemist, Charles Bromley, who told him that a young man had entered his shop at 6.30 pm, and had asked for forty grains of hydrate of chloral. Mr Bromley asked for a prescription, which the customer did not have. However, he insisted that he needed it for his mother, who was suffering from angina pectoris. The chemist agreed to provide him with a smaller amount, but the young man reached over the counter and grabbed the hydrate of chloride before running out of the shop.

Caminada had interviewed several witnesses and now had some idea of the description of the young man he was looking for. He was somewhere in the region of 5ft 2ins to 5ft 4ins in height; he was clean shaven; and he was wearing either a light brown or light check suit. This was relatively little to go on, but he had a major break when he was able to trace the man who had alerted the cab driver that the individual had jumped out of the cab. The witness informed the detective, that after doing so he had run towards the area of All Saints' Church, and armed with this additional information, Caminada made enquiries in that district.

One of the places he made enquiries at was a beerhouse called the *York Minster,* on Higher Chatham Street. Here, the landlord, Andrew Holt, described how the young man had arrived around 7 pm on the night in question. He recalled that he was wearing a gold watch and chain, which he remembered he had pulled out of his pocket to check the time. He ordered soda and milk and when paying, took out a large amount of money. This information was corroborated by Emily Pearson

The victim is lifted from the cab after reaching hospital, but it was too late as he died moments later. The Illustrated Police News

and her daughter Mary Ann, who had been working in the beerhouse that night. The customer had asked for a cab to be ordered on his behalf, and fortunately for the detective, the cabman was known to them.

His name was William Coleman, and Caminada wasted no time in locating him. He remembered the young man very well, and having agreed a fare of 1s 6d [7.5 p], he took him to the *Locomotive Inn* on Oldham road. The pieces of the jigsaw were beginning to fall into place, as Caminada knew the place and its landlord, John Parton, also known as 'Pig Jack,' well. Before taking over the *Locomotive Inn* he had run a notorious beerhouse in Greengate, Salford. He was well-known amongst Manchester's boxing fraternity, and it was rumoured that he had been known to put a drug in the water used for washing out the mouths of the opponents of the fighters he had backed. Furthermore, he was also said to have spiked the drinks of some of his customers to rob them. Clearly, John Parton did not fit the description of John Fletcher's companion, but Caminada reasoned that perhaps one of his sons had decided to use this knowledge of the use of drugs as an aid to robbery.

One in particular matched the description of the individual Caminada was keen to interview, and that was eighteen-year-old Charles Parton. He was traced to 12 Moor Street, off Rochdale Road, and at 12.30 am on the morning of 2 March, Caminada and his colleague, Inspector Wilson, went to the house and arrested the suspect.

Charles Parton was born in 1869, and after a little education, became a messenger in a Manchester hotel. However, he did not keep this job for long and since then he had had little experience of work. His father had been described as the 9st 4lb champion of England, and Charles also showed some expertise in boxing, and spent a brief spell in America, where he tried to make some headway in the sport. He also had a criminal record, having been convicted of stealing from a hotel in Market Harborough, for which he received a six months prison sentence. He had also been convicted of defrauding a railway company at Stockport.

A number of identity parades were held, and several witnesses helped place the young man at the Cathedral, in the

Three Arrows, jumping from the cab, in the *York Minster,* being taken by cab to the *Locomotive Inn,* and also as the person who stole the chloral from the chemist's shop in Liverpool. Witnesses were also able to provide details of when the victim had been in possession of his cash and valuables, and that some of these items were subsequently seen in Parton's possession. The young man was charged initially with having stolen from the person of John Fletcher, a gold watch and chain valued at £120, and an unknown sum of money. Parton declared himself to be innocent and told the detective that he had been at a coursing meeting in Liverpool that day, and had returned home at 6 pm, after which he had stayed indoors.

On the morning of 4 March, Parton was brought before the city police court charged with robbery, and also on suspicion of having caused the death of John Fletcher. The stipendiary magistrate, Mr F J Headlam, further remanded him in custody.

The huge amount of public and press interest proved to be of immense help to Caminada, as two apparent earlier victims of Parton contacted him. On 8 January 1889, Samuel Oldfield of Ashton visited Manchester and had met a young man. Mr Oldfield was later found in a stupefied and apparently drunken state, minus his watch valued at £10 and his cash. At the time, the police did not believe his story of possibly being drugged by a young man and he was brought before Mr Headlam the following morning and received a fine for being drunk.

Another who came forward was John Parkey, who on 28 December 1888, had been robbed of his watch and chain together with some cash, after apparently being drugged. Each of them identified the prisoner, and revenge must have tasted sweet to them both.

Parton's trial opened on Monday, 18 March 1889, at St George's Hall, Liverpool, and he faced a charge of murdering John Fletcher and of stealing his property: he was also charged with additional matters relating to Samuel Oldfield and John Parkey. The trial was notable as it was the first case in which chloral had allegedly been used to murder a victim, although it had long been suspected that it had been used in robberies in the past. Mr Justice Charles was the trial judge and the prosecution was conducted by Mr Hopwood and Mr Shee, with Mr McKeand and Mr Jordan acting on behalf of the accused.

The prosecution team had been well served by Caminada, who had provided them with a more or less open and shut case. He had found witnesses who could place the prisoner and victim together at relevant times; he had provided two other victims, indicating an established pattern of behaviour: there was evidence of the prisoner obtaining chloral and Caminada had also discovered that the prisoner's father had been treated for angina pretoris, which was the complaint described by the thief of the chloral.

However, Caminada had not been satisfied with this, and in the days leading up to the trial he had discovered a new witness, who had seen Parton put a liquid into a glass of beer at the *Three Arrows,* whilst the prisoner was in the company of John Fletcher. The new witness was a respectable bookkeeper, named Andrew Phillips, who had not come forward initially as he did not wish his employers or his wife to know that he frequented an establishment with the reputation of the *Three Arrows,* even though he had read about the case and knew he had vital evidence. Eventually, he raised it with his employers, and it is they who seemingly contacted Caminada.

The defence naturally attempted to discredit him, but Phillips, although an unwilling witness was a plausible and devastating one. He was adamant in his claims and when asked why nobody else in such a busy bar room had witnessed the event he described, he was able to explain that his seat was the only vantage point from which it could have been seen.

The defence called no witnesses and did not attempt to suggest that their client had not been the young man seen with the deceased on the night in question. They called on the jury to be cautious about convicting Parton due to the fact that this was the first trial where the drug had been given as the method of murder, and they argued that alcohol was more likely to have been the cause of death, as John Fletcher was known to have been a heavy drinker.

In his summing up, the judge reminded the jury that if they believed that the prisoner had administered chloral, and this had brought forward the victim's death, it was wilful murder.

The Three Arrows, Deansgate.

The Three Arrows, *one of Manchester's most notorious pubs.* The Manchester Evening Chronicle

This was the rightful verdict even if they believed Parton had not intended to kill the victim. If they were not satisfied that this was the case, they should find him not guilty.

The jury retired and it was at this stage that Parton revealed what the press described as his cool and calculating character, even though he was only eighteen-years-old. As he clearly realised he would be convicted, and whatever the sentence proved to be, he realised that he would have to eat a poor and very strict diet for a few weeks until his execution or for many years if he was reprieved. He had therefore asked for some friends to club together to buy what would perhaps be his last slap-up meal, and as the jury retired, he calmly went down into the cells to eat it.

He had to eat it very quickly, as the jury returned after just twenty minutes, with a guilty verdict, but with a strong recommendation for mercy. The judge sentenced him to death in the normal manner and warned him that he could not guarantee that the jury's recommendation would be agreed to, and rather ominously, he warned the prisoner to prepare himself for death. As he had been found guilty in the Fletcher case, all charges relating to Oldfield and Parkey were dropped.

Controversy surrounding this case continued in the trial's aftermath, as his family desperately sought to gain a reprieve. There was some speculation about a missing witness, to whom the prisoner had allegedly confessed before the trial. Furthermore, doubt was cast on the validity of the city analyst's evidence regarding the significance of chloral, which went to the heart of the prosecution case, and raised the question as to whether the murder had actually occurred.

As far as the alleged missing witness was concerned, there was press speculation that a friend of the Parton family, John Whittaker, had visited the prisoner as he awaited trial. During that visit it was said that Parton had made some incriminating remarks. Apparently he had said that he knew John Fletcher from when the youngster had previously worked in the city centre hotel. The older man had sometimes stayed there, and on 26 February, they had got into conversation, and they agreed to have a drink together. Parton had indeed intended to drug and rob him, but quickly realised he had given him too much and that he was 'a gonner.' He had returned to the cab with the specific intention of jumping out as soon as possible.

John Whittaker is said to have made no secret about what was said and this was rumoured to have reached the ears of Detective Caminada, who unsuccessfully attempted to locate him and issue him with a subpoena, requiring him to give evidence. The prisoner and his family strenuously denied this at the time, and in his memoirs, Caminada makes no mention of it.

This case had not only generated much interest in the press and amongst the general public, for it did so within medical and scientific circles. A Dr Gumbert of Manchester wrote an attack of the city analyst's findings, which was published in the *British Medical Journal,* shortly after the trial ended. Dr Gumbert was adamant that a murder had not taken place, and he criticised the criminal justice system, which he claimed had literally rushed to judgement, pointing out that from the moment of John Fletcher's death to the sentence of death being imposed, insufficient time had elapsed to have allowed for an adequate scientific investigation to have taken place. He continued by saying that he considered it wholly inappropriate for only one chemical analysis to have been made. However, even if reliance was put on Charles Estcourt's findings, the trace of chloral was not sufficient to have caused or contributed in any way to the death of John Fletcher, who was more likely to have died of alcohol poisoning.

Charles Estcourt wrote a rebuttal, and the views of Dr Gumbert were published too late to have a bearing on the trial. However, his article had raised some serious doubts about the case, and as a result, several politicians wrote to Parton's solicitors, in support of a reprieve. The MPs who wrote in support included Mr C E Schwann, Mr Jacob Bright, Mr Addison QC, and Sir William Houldsworth. In all, more than 3,000 signatures were collected in Manchester and Liverpool in support of a reprieve, and his solicitor, Mr William Burton, presented the petition personally to the Home Secretary in early April.

The trial judge had in fact supported the jury's recommendation for mercy and his youth, together with the widespread belief that he had not intended to kill the victim, combined to make a persuasive case for a reprieve. However, there remained a substantial section of the press and public who believed that a reprieve would send out the wrong message to others who might be tempted to use drugs in robberies, and that this was a case in which a deterrent sentence was called for.

A reprieve was by no means inevitable, as on Saturday, 6 April, his father, mother and six siblings left Manchester at

Three of the Members of Parliament who gave their names to the attempt to save the killer from the gallows: Jacob Bright [above], *Charles E Schwann* [above, right], *and Sir William Houldsworth* [below]. Manchester Old and New

11.30 am. As they awaited their train to Liverpool, a railway policeman approached them on the platform and expressed his relief that their son had been granted a reprieve and he had just read the news in a newspaper. The Parton family did not believe him, as they had heard nothing, and continued on their journey. Upon their arrival at Kirkdale gaol at 2.30 pm, where their son was being held and the execution was due to take place, a warder confirmed that their son had indeed been granted a reprieve. Only his mother and father were allowed to see him, and when he appeared he was in different prison clothes. He had not been told of the reprieve and assumed they were the clothes he would be hanged and buried in.

Charles Parton had been described as callous, cool and calculating, but when told of his reprieve by his parents, he broke down and wept uncontrollably. On leaving the prison, John Parton gave an impromptu press conference, and expressed his thanks to the governor and the staff for the kindness they had shown their son and themselves. He had told his parents as he began his life sentence, that one day, if he was released, he would like to travel to the American West.

Caminada's memoirs were published whilst Parton was still in prison, and the detective noted that a few months after the trial, John Parkey died of the effects of being drugged by Charles Parton.

CHAPTER 11

The Crumpsall Workhouse Outrage 1900

On 23 April 1900, Charlotte Southgate, of Ryder Street, Crumpsall, took her thirty-seven-year-old husband, Francis, to the local workhouse. A packer by trade, Francis, who had been diagnosed an 'imbecile', was also suffering from spinal paralysis. His condition had been deteriorating during the previous twelve months, and Charlotte was no longer able to cope with the demands of caring for him. The workhouse was a last resort, and this was to be a temporary arrangement only, for as soon as his condition improved, he could return home to her.

She visited him each month, which was the maximum workhouse regulations allowed. When she did so on 1 September, she found him to be quite ill, and furthermore, he had a black eye. When she questioned him about it he made no complaint, but as she was leaving, he begged her to take him home with her. Unfortunately, he was not yet well enough, and as she bade him goodbye, she was unaware that this was to be the last time she would see him alive: nor could she have realised that her husband's death would lead to a massive scandal, as it would lead to a workhouse and its administration being opened to public scrutiny.

In the early hours of 3 October, Dr JC Muir, resident medical officer to the Crumpsall Workhouse, was wakened by George Prescott, a night attendant on the imbecile ward. Prescott advised the doctor that Francis Southgate had just died. Dr Muir made a few cursory enquiries of Prescott, and issued a death certificate citing 'paralysis of the insane' as the primary cause of death, and a secondary cause as cardiac syncope. This was done without leaving his bedroom and inspecting the body. Prescott returned to the ward, where he laid out the body in preparation for its disposal, as Dr Muir returned to his bed.

Francis John Headlam was appointed the city's Stipendary Magistrate in April 1869, and held the post for several years, during which time many of Manchester's criminals appeared before him, including George Prescott. Manchester Old and New

Matters would have rested there had not two inmate helpers on the night wards, James Tattersall and William Naylor, taken the brave decision to report what they had seen to the workhouse superintendent. This was only after they had thought about it all of the following day, as they were in a vulnerable position within the workhouse, with no standing whatsoever. Nevertheless, they decided that they had no option, and as soon as they had told the superintendent, Mr J T Roberts, he passed the information on to the workhouse master, Major Ballantyne, who in turn contacted the Manchester police. The two men had advised the superintendent and the workhouse master that they had witnessed Prescott strangle Southgate.

When Prescott reported for duty, he was confronted and at 6 am on 4 October he was arrested for the wilful murder of Francis Southgate. He was produced before the stipendary magistrate, Mr Headlam, at the city police court later that morning, when Superintendent McKenzie, of the Manchester police, gave an outline of the case. As a result, the accused was remanded in custody until the following day, when the inquest was to be held.

The inquest was held by Mr Smelt, the city coroner, and those in attendance included the following interested spectators: Mr G Rooke, chairman of the Manchester Board of Guardians, another board member, Mr Alderman McDonagh, and from the Crumpsall Workhouse, Mr Watmough, vice chairman of the governing committee, and its master, Major Ballantyne. These worthy gentlemen must have felt extremely uncomfortable as they waited for the proceedings to begin and their unease can only have intensified as the hearing progressed.

Formal evidence was taken from Charlotte Southgate regarding her late husband's history of ill health, and his more recent spell in the workhouse. Next, Dr Muir was called to give evidence.

The crime caused a sensation when it was announced in the press. Manchester Evening News.

ALLEGED
FIENDISH OUTRAGE
AT
CRUMPSALL WORKHOUSE.

INMATE STRANGLED TO DEATH

ATTENDANT CHARGED WITH MURDER.

A shocking tragedy which occurred in the Crumpsall Workhouse early yesterday morning was brought to light at the Manchester City Police Court this morning, when a night attendant named George Prescott was charged with the wilful murder of an imbecile inmate named Francis Southgate. According to the evidence which came to the knowledge of the Manchester police yesterday, the prisoner was on night duty in the early hours of yesterday morning. He was apparently annoyed by the noisy conduct of Southgate. In order to silence him the prisoner, it is alleged, threw a towel round the imbecile's neck and twisted it tightly. Not satisfied with this, he got a poker, and using it as a tourniquet

He began by confirming that he had been responsible for the deceased's medical care since July, and that he had been diagnosed as suffering from general paralysis and insanity. Dr Muir acknowledged that he had seen him frequently, but only when passing his bed, but he had not been called to treat him for any reason during his stay. He was, however, aware that his medical condition was deteriorating and that he had gained this information by word of mouth from the ward staff. He had also heard that he could be troublesome, but he had not been called to him for that reason, namely to authorise his being tied down to the bed. At this point, Dr Muir appeared to become increasingly agitated, and felt it necessary to remind the court that there were more than 150 similar patients for whom he had responsibility, and he could not be too specific. On further questioning he agreed that he had last seen him, but without examining him, on Tuesday, 2 October, at the regular quarterly review of all patients. At that time, Southgate was confined to his bed, but there were no complaints about his conduct.

The coroner then focused his questioning on the events surrounding the death of the patient. Dr Muir recalled being advised by Prescott that Southgate had been taken ill very suddenly and died, which was said to have occurred in Prescott's presence. Dr Muir wrote out the death certificate, and he confirmed that he had not viewed the body until some hours later, in the presence of Dr Heslop, the police surgeon. An incredulous coroner questioned the witness further about his behaviour at the time:

Coroner: Did you not make any further inquiry or examination?

Muir: I had seen the man the previous day. The interest would have been purely scientific if I had made a post-mortem examination. I was very busy at the time, and did not think it was necessary to make a post-mortem. Deaths of this kind frequently happened.

Coroner: Do you mean to say that you gave a certificate without verifying it or making any inquiry at all?

Muir: Yes. I had seen him the previous day.

Coroner: I do not intend to make any remarks about it now, although I am very much astonished to hear you say so. It is not a matter to go into here. You afterwards gave a certificate that death was due to cardiac syncope and general paralysis of the insane. What do you say now was the cause of death?

Muir: I believe now, after the examination with Dr Heslop, that death was due to asphyxia induced by strangulation. There is only one other possibility that I can see. From what was found, there must have been considerable violence used, and death might have been due to shock.

Coroner: Whether it was from asphyxia or shock, do you agree that death was the result of violence?

Muir: Yes

Coroner: You saw this man in good health one morning, and it was reported to you the next morning that he was dead. Did you not go and see him?

Muir: It did not occur to me to go and see him. I saw the body about fifteen hours afterwards. I did not consider it worthwhile to see the body.

Coroner: At the same time, he was well the day before?

Muir: What was I to do?

Evidence about the hours immediately preceding Southgate's death was provided by an inmate of the workhouse, who also acted as a helper to the full time staff within the institution. This was James Tattersall, a crucial witness, who was working on the ward in question, with Prescott, at the time of the death.

Tattersall reported for night duty, as usual at 7 pm, on Tuesday, 2 October, on the male imbecile ward, where he found Prescott already at work, and at this stage, Southgate was quiet. Quite apart from the thirteen men on their ward, the two men were also responsible for a large number of other men on nearby wards.

At 9.30 pm, Southgate became very noisy, shouting loudly and defying Prescott who shouted 'Are you going to stop it?' To which he received the reply 'No I am not.' Prescott got on the bed, and held Southgate down by his arms as he knelt on

James Tatersall gives his crucial evidence at Prescott's trial. The Manchester Evening Chronicle

his chest. The two men continued to struggle and fell to the floor. Another full time member of staff, Walter Hurst, who had heard the commotion from a nearby ward, approached the two struggling men. He held the patient down by the legs as Prescott grabbed him by the throat. After a few minutes, Hurst said to Prescott 'That will do. You have done enough.' Both attendants rose to their feet, which allowed the now subdued Southgate the opportunity of returning to his bed.

All was quiet for a while, but one hour later Southgate again became agitated and noisy. Prescott attempted to quieten him by holding him down on the bed, and after a brief struggle he again grabbed Southgate by the throat. They both fell to the floor again, and Southgate rolled under his bed in an attempt to escape from the other man. However, Prescott pulled him out from his place of shelter, knelt on his chest, and said to Tattersall 'Fetch me a towel and we will quieten this man.' Tattersall took a towel from a medicine chest and took it over to Prescott, who rolled it up like a scarf before putting it around Southgate's neck, and twisting it tightly, saying 'He cannot shout so well now.'

This continued for about five minutes, before the grip was loosened, thus allowing Southgate to return to his bed. He remained still for another hour, before again rising, but after rearranging his sheets he got back into bed. At 3.15am, he began shouting again, and this would prove to be the last occasion he would do so.

Prescott approached him and demanded 'Are you going to hold your noise?' Southgate's response was a defiant 'No I am not.' Prescott took him by the throat and again they fell to the floor. The attendant grabbed the towel, which lay next to them, and tied the two ends together as he held the other man down. He then looped it around Southgate's neck, who shouted 'I've had enough Mr Prescott, you will hear about this.' In response, Prescott simply tightened the towel even more, before asking Tattersall to hand him a poker, which lay in the nearby fire place. Tattersall did so before sitting down in a chair by the fire place, from which he claimed to have had a clear view of what happened during the following minutes.

He testified that he saw Prescott twist the poker around the towel at the back of Southgate's neck, as though it was a tourniquet, as the unfortunate victim made horrible croaking and gurgling sounds. Eventually, after several minutes, Prescott removed the poker, which was described as now being bent, followed by the towel. It was obvious, however, that something was dreadfully wrong, which led Prescott to exclaim 'Good God, the man is dead. I will go for the doctor.' The two men lifted Southgate back onto the bed, and although he moved a little he soon became quite still.

Prescott left the ward to seek out the resident doctor, and upon his return fifteen minutes later, he assured Tattersall that he had seen Dr Muir and everything was 'all right.' At 5.30 am, Prescott went to rouse the workhouse superintendent, Mr Roberts, to advise him of the death. The superintendent confirmed that the doctor had been told, and being content with the affirmative reply, he did not consider it necessary to pursue the matter any further.

At the close of his evidence, he was open to questioning, and Major Ballantyne asked him to confirm to the coroner that he had worked as an inmate helper for seven years and had never seen a poker used in a similar manner in the past, which Tattersall fortunately was able to do so. During his evidence he had mentioned that Southgate only ever became distressed in the presence of the accused man, and an astute member of the coroner's jury asked him to confirm this, which he did.

Walter Hurst told the hearing that he had heard a disturbance and left his own place of work to see what was happening. He agreed that he had assisted in attempting to control the inmate by holding him down by his legs at one stage, as he believed the accused was having genuine difficulty in controlling him. When asked by the coroner if staff should not deal with troublesome inmates in a better manner, the witness replied 'You cannot let them do what they like.'

William Naylor was the next witness to take the stand, and he confirmed that he too was an inmate helper on the night wards, and had been on duty at the time of Southgate's death. He denied actually seeing the event itself but on closer questioning by the coroner, he had to acknowledge that from Prescott's actions he had assumed that he was going to strangle the victim. When asked by the coroner if he could not have tried to prevent it happening, he replied that 'It was none of my business.'

Dr Heslop, the police surgeon, gave details of the post-mortem examination, namely that death had been due to asphyxia, caused by strangulation. He had found marks on the neck similar to those which would be expected to occur if a towel had been used. Having heard Dr Heslop and considered the earlier evidence, the coroner's jury returned with a verdict of wilful murder by the prisoner, who was committed to the Manchester Autumn Assizes at his next appearance before the stipendary magistrate, Mr Headlam, on 9 October.

The enormity of the scandal in which they and their institution were enmeshed, was recognised by the members of the Manchester Board of Guardians, who met on Wednesday, 17 October, under the chairmanship of Mr G Rooke. They were all aware of the issues that the case had raised in public view, and in an attempt to minimise the impact of the revelations, they released details of their deliberations to the press.

They emphasised the great care that was taken in recruiting staff, and that Prescott had had to submit three testimonials when he applied for his position. The board members also noted increases in staff numbers in the recent past and also that wages had been raised to encourage a better quality of applicant. They also felt that the public ought to be made aware of the very serious shortage of spaces in the lunatic asylums, where individuals such as Southgate ought to be, and that the workhouse was not intended to deal with troublesome and violent lunatics. For the past two or three years there had been no spaces in the local asylums, and the police had regularly brought such individuals to the workhouse door, as there was nowhere else for them to go. Three years earlier, plans had been made to build another asylum, but these had to be abandoned due to economic reasons. The meeting was also able to confirm that William Hurst had resigned.

Prescott's trial took place on 14 November, before Mr Justice Darling, and the courtroom was packed as the prisoner entered the dock to state his not guilty plea. Mr McKeand and Mr Pope prosecuted, and the prisoner was represented by Mr Byrne.

Much of the evidence was similar to that already heard at the inquest, and the jury was advised that Prescott had accepted a measure of responsibility for what had occurred, from the very beginning. When initially confronted by Major Ballantyne, he had said ' I am afraid I did use unnecessary

The Manchester Assize Courts, where Prescott stood trial. Manchester Faces and Places

violence by seizing him by the throat. I lost my temper.' However, he had always strenuously denied using the poker and towel in the manner described by other witnesses. This became the central issue of the trial, as the defence could more easily claim that the patient's death had been an accident or at worse, manslaughter, if only the accused's hands had been used.

The defence attempted to highlight inconsistencies in Tattersall's evidence, and also suggested that there was some malice directed towards the accused, but this was strongly denied. The court also heard from the hapless Dr Muir, who by now had resigned his position as resident medical officer to Crumpsall Workhouse.

The evidence of Dr Heslop was recognised by all of the involved parties as being crucially important. He described his findings from the post-mortem examination of 4 October, and confirmed that the marks on the neck, in his opinion, could not have been caused by use of the hands only, and were the result of twisted cloth being used. Other marks on the neck were caused by fingers and thumbs. The cause of death was suffocation by strangulation with violence, and in his opinion the marks were consistent with the details provided by Tattersall regarding the towel and poker. However, under cross examination, he conceded that the marks could possibly have been caused by the victim's own collar as he was being strangled.

The defence also called an attendant at the workhouse as a witness, who confirmed that the poker had in fact been in its present bent condition for several months before Southgate's death. This contradicted Tattersall's evidence, that it had been straight when he had handed it to the accused on the night of the crime.

However, Mr Byrne's main witness was to be Mr Joseph Collier, a surgeon at the Royal Infirmary, and lecturer in surgery at Owens College. Despite his impressive credentials, he was to be of little help to the defence. Dr Collier began by stating that in his view it was impossible to determine whether the marks on the deceased's neck were caused by a towel or fingers. Before he could make any further progress with his evidence, the judge asked him if had actually seen the body as Dr Heslop had done. Dr Collier advised the judge that he had not done so, but he had read Dr Heslop's notes. On hearing this, the judge ordered him out of the witness box before he could give any further opinions.

Mr Byrne suggested to the jury that even if credence was given to evidence that described a towel and poker being used, it still did not mean that his client intended to kill Southgate but it had been used as a desperate means of controlling a difficult and violent man. He urged the members of the jury to bear in mind the evidence, albeit brief due to the intervention of the judge, of Dr Collier. He concluded by stating that it would be unfair on the defendant if they placed too much reliance on the evidence provided by Tattersall and also Naylor, who had given evidence during the trial, presumably as they were inmates.

In his summing up, the judge advised the jury that only two verdicts were possible, murder or manslaughter. If the prisoner had been unable to control Southgate, he should have sought permission from the superintendent and Dr Muir to fasten him down to his bed by his hands and feet, which was workhouse policy. Furthermore, he had by his own admission accepted that he had used violence. As for the evidence of Tattersall and Naylor, the defence had not provided any substantial reason as to why their testimonies should be discounted.

Justice Darling next turned his attention to Dr Muir, who should have gone to see the body but did not do so. He accused him of putting his own slumbers above the needs of an inmate in his care, for which he was paid.

George Prescott in the dock as he faces trial for the murder of Francis Southgate. The Manchester Evening Chronicle

Prescott had gone to the doctor and told him the man was dead, but what, asked the judge, if he had not in fact been dead; could he have been saved by the doctor?

A clearly distressed Dr Muir, who was in court, interrupted the judge by shouting 'I asked him if he was sure he was dead and he said 'Yes'.' The judge retorted angrily 'Asked this man, the man charged with murder!'

As for the towel and poker, the jury could still return with a murder verdict, if they thought they had not been used, as the prisoner had no right to grab the victim by the throat, even if only using his hands.

The jury retired at 5 pm and returned forty minutes later, having found Prescott guilty of manslaughter. In sentencing him, the judge reminded the prisoner that he had killed an unfortunate and defenceless man, who had been placed in his care. He continued by stating that it was 'as near to murder as anything could be.' However, he accepted that Prescott had been in an extremely difficult position, with responsibility for far too many patients, many of whom should have been in a more suitable institution. This was not an excuse, but it would be taken into account in determining sentence. If it had not been for these exceptional circumstances he would have received a much heavier sentence than the seven years penal servitude imposed.

Francis Southgate died as a result of an individual act of cruelty, for which his assailant was punished. However, he died in an institution which itself was put on trial as much as the individual concerned. It is little wonder that workhouses were dreaded by the poor of the Victorian age, and fortunately their days were numbered.

Shortly after the trial ended, the government announced that as from 1 December 1900, the death of any lunatic in any poor law institution must be reported to the local coroner within forty-eight hours of death occurring.

The case had attracted a great deal of public interest, and a major question that was being asked in many quarters was just how many inmates of workhouses had met similarly cruel ends within their walls.

CHAPTER 12

The Strange Tale of Mrs Bland's Skull
1900

The Manchester Autumn Assizes of 1900 was one of the busiest for years, and four murder trials were listed amongst the cases to be heard. One of these was held on Monday, 12 November, when fifty-four-year-old Henry Bland was accused of killing his wife, Hannah, at their home, 30 Bury Street, Gorton, on 13 July earlier the same year.

The trial judge was Mr Justice Darling, and the prosecution was led by Mr Kershaw. Bland's defence was undertaken by Mr McKeand. On entering the dock, he wore a shabby brown suit and a collarless shirt, which added to his haggard appearance, although when asked for his plea, he answered in a loud, clear voice 'Not guilty.'

The events which had led to this trial, occurred four months earlier, in the couple's home, where they lived with their two children, twenty-six-year-old Michael, a boilerman, and fourteen-year-old Hannah. On the morning of 13 July, Michael, left for work at 10 am, and was soon followed out of the house by young Hannah. The prisoner asked his wife to make him a basin of gruel, which she did, and placed it on the table at 11.30 am. Thirty minutes later, Bland asked a young boy, Albert Atkinson to fetch him a gill of beer. When Albert returned with it a few minutes later, Bland went back into the house, and the youngster heard the sound of the door being bolted from the inside.

About five minutes later, Albert heard the door being unbolted, and saw Mrs Bland come out of the house, with her head covered in blood. She asked him to fetch her neighbour, Mrs Frost, who on arrival took Mrs Bland back into the house. There was no sign of Mr Bland, who had left by the front door, and made his way to Gorton police station, where he stated 'I have murdered my wife at 30 Bury Street and I have come to give myself up.'

He was detained at the police station, as Constable Edwards went to the house. Here, he bathed the victim's head wound, and noted that she was covered in gruel. He called for Dr W Robertson, who treated her at home and stitched the wound. He thought that it was superficial, especially as Mrs Bland told him that it had been caused by her husband throwing the basin of gruel at her, which hit her on the back of the head.

At the police station, Bland was charged with unlawfully wounding his wife, having used the basin as a weapon against her. On being charged he replied 'I did strike her on the head.' On 17 July, he appeared before the stipendiary magistrate, Mr Yates, by which time the charge had been reduced in seriousness to one of aggravated assault. This was largely due to the evidence given at the hearing by the victim, who again stated that the basin had been the weapon that her husband had used. No medical evidence was given, as it was not considered necessary, and Mr Yates sentenced Bland to six months imprisonment with hard labour.

The case would normally have concluded there and then, had it not been for a deterioration in Mrs Bland's condition, which led to Dr Robertson again being called to treat her. He attempted to persuade her to enter hospital, not just so that she could receive medical treatment, but also so that she would be removed from the squalid and insanitary conditions in which she was living in the family

THE PRISONER
(A SKETCH IN COURT)

Henry Bland in the dock at his trial for the murder of his wife. The Manchester Evening Chronicle

home. These were hindering her progress, but she refused to leave and go to the hospital. She later seemed to change her mind and arrangements were made to admit her into the Chorlton Union Hospital on 24 July. However, when hospital staff came to collect her, she refused to go with them. She subsequently died on 5 August, and a post mortem was carried out by Dr R D Gunn, the results of which were to have a dramatic impact on the case.

The post-mortem revealed that the scalp was in a very unhealthy state, and on the surface of the head, he found a depression and severe bruising. Pieces of the fractured skull had pressed against blood vessels which leaked blood, leading to progressive paralysis, which was the cause of death. Dr Gunn had immediately noticed the extraordinary thickness of the victim's skull, which meant that a high level of violence would have had to be used to cause the damage to it. It was thus, highly unlikely that a basin thrown from a distance of a few feet could have been the cause.

This information led the police to make further enquiries and to make another search of the Blands' home. This revealed the existence of an axe, kept for chopping firewood. It was noted that there was a piece missing from the blade, and when fitted against the skull, there was a perfect match.

As a result of these developments, Sergeant Davies visited Bland in Strangeways prison on 7 August, and having advised him of his wife's death, told him he would be charged with causing it. Bland replied 'Is that so?' When formally charged with her murder on 20 August he made no reply.

When he entered the dock at the Assizes on the morning of his trial, it was only after an unusual series of events. He was still serving the six months prison sentence, imposed by the stipendiary magistrate. This was for an offence which had only been reduced in the level of seriousness following the testimony of his wife, at that hearing. He faced a charge of murdering that same victim, but with using a different weapon to that which Mrs Bland had said that he had used against her.

The first two witnesses for the prosecution were the Bland children. Michael's testimony confirmed the long standing volatile nature of his parents' relationship during their thirty years of marriage. His father had left his job with Messrs Beyer, Peacock and Co a fortnight before the crime, and had been drinking more heavily than usual. His mother was by no means a drunkard, but Michael acknowledged that she drank regularly. The week before the assault, he had heard his father say to Mrs Bland, 'You ought to be dead. I can easily get a better woman than you anyway.'

The accused's daughter, Hannah, gives evidence against her father at his trial.
The Manchester Evening Chronicle

Young Hannah appeared next, and her evidence highlighted the significance of the axe. She confirmed that during the evening prior to the crime, her father had been drinking heavily and was 'Drunk as a mop' by the time he went to bed at 6 pm. She further advised the court that on the afternoon of 13 July, after the assault had occurred, she had found the axe behind a chair in the parlour. This was unusual, as she had never seen it inside the house before, as it was always kept on the coal pile in the back yard. She had used it the previous day to chop wood for the fire.

Hannah's testimony raises several questions, the first of which was why was the axe not mentioned previously. True, her mother had stated that the basin had been used as the weapon, which Mrs Bland may well have believed to be so, and the young girl may not have realised its significance. However, Bland had left the house almost immediately to go to the police station, and it is unlikely that he would have stopped to clean the axe, as there was little point in doing so given his admission to the police. It is possible that Hannah had found the axe covered in her mother's blood and hair. Not realising the deadly nature of her wound, had Mrs Bland colluded with her daughter in an attempt to minimise the seriousness of the charge Bland was to face. Young Hannah may have been so persuaded and it was only after her mother's death that she became upset with her father for causing it. We will never know.

As a nine-year-old, the judge had to satisfy himself that Albert Atkinson was competent to give evidence, and before he could do so, Mr Justice Darling asked him some probing questions. Albert coped well and told the judge that he had been taught at school that if he did not tell the truth he would be caned. The judge asked if he had been taught that he might be punished by someone else if he lied. Albert replied 'Yes God.' The judge smiled and said 'Kiss the Book.' Albert's evidence was important in that he gave details of giving beer to the accused, hearing the door being bolted, and later, of seeing Mrs Bland emerge from the house, with blood on her head.

Dr Gunn was called to give his evidence, which he did in a most dramatic manner. He advised the court of the findings of his post-mortem, and his realisation that the basin, which although may have been thrown at the victim, could not have caused the injuries to Mrs Bland's skull. The discovery of the axe had been hugely significant, and he now held it in his hand. In his other hand he held the lower portion of Mrs Bland's skull. For the benefit of the jury he lined up the wound with the axe blade, to reveal the perfect fit, as the notch fitted in exactly with the wound.

The judge wished to ensure that the jury members should know exactly which part of the skull was being held by Dr Gunn. The witness attempted to line it up using his own head, but in trying to reach behind himself, found it difficult to do so, and this problem was overcome in a most unusual manner. The High Sheriff was sat on the bench alongside the judge, close to the witness box. He assisted Dr Gunn by leaning over and allowing the doctor to place Mrs Bland's skull against his own.

Dr Heslop, divisional police surgeon, was the next witness and he agreed in full with Dr Gunn's findings. He further stated that the wound had been inflicted by someone wielding the axe from behind and slightly to the right of the victim.

Mr J F Price, county coroner, then read out the statement made by the prisoner at his wife's inquest. Bland had accused his wife of being a hard drinker, which had caused many difficulties in their marriage. As a result of this, he had enlisted in the army in1881 and was away from her for seven years. He had served in the Highland Light Infantry and was decorated during the Egyptian campaign, in which he saw active service, but eventually had returned home. He had concluded by stating that on 13 July they had quarrelled about the gruel, and he had thrown the basin at her, which he insisted had caused her to fall to the floor, which was the cause of her death.

After the prosecution concluded their case, the defence called no other witnesses. Instead Mr McKeand attempted to persuade the jury to find his client guilty of manslaughter and not murder. He emphasised the fact that the victim herself had not mentioned the axe. This, he proposed, meant that there was doubt about which weapon had actually been used. Clearly, if the jury could be persuaded that death resulted from his client simply throwing the basin, this was more likely to result in a manslaughter conviction, than if they believed that he had deliberately struck her violently from behind, which could only result in a murder conviction.

In his summing up, however, Mr Justice Darling asked the jury if any reasonable person could agree that after examining the skull, that the wound could possibly have been caused by a basin being thrown at the victim. He noted that the prisoner was not said to be drunk when he surrendered himself to the police, and although he had drunk a gill of beer, he presumably was not at the time of the assault. The prisoner had not mentioned the basin until the hearing before the stipendiary magistrate, and he may well have decided to take advantage of the victim's evidence, in which the axe was not mentioned. The judge instructed the jury to dismiss from their minds the fact that Bland was already serving a prison sentence for assaulting her. Furthermore, it was immaterial that the victim had neglected to take care of herself and refused to enter hospital.

The jury returned after thirty minutes, with a conviction for murder, but with a strong recommendation for mercy. After

THE GORTON MURDER.

SKETCHES IN COURT.

MR JUSTICE DARLING
PASSES THE
EXTREME PENALTY

MR McKEAND FOR
THE PRISONER

THE JAVELIN MAN

The judge dons the black cap to pass the death sentence, following the verdict, which was guilty despite the best efforts of his barrister, Mr McKeand. The javelin men were old-time court officers, who accompanied senior judges. The Manchester Evening Chronicle

placing the black cap on his head, the judge asked the prisoner if he had anything to say. Bland repeated his claim by saying 'I never used an axe.'

To this, the judge replied 'Your statement that you did not use the axe on your wife, no one will credit. It is perfectly plain that the axe caused the injury from which she died.' He then sentenced him to death.

The Home Secretary was petitioned by his legal representatives, and on 22 November Mr R D Cruikshank, governor of Strangeways prison, advised Bland that he had been granted a reprieve. The prisoner was said to be 'much relieved and grateful.' Arrangements were then put in place to transfer him to a penal settlement to begin his life sentence.

Sources and Bibliography

Bent, Superintendent James, *Criminal Life-Reminiscences of Forty-Two Years as a Police Officer*

Caminada, Jerome, *Twenty-Five Years of Detective Life Vols I & II*, Jerome Caminada, 1901

The *Illustrated Police News*

Manchester Evening News

The *Manchester Guardian*

The *Manchester Courier*

The *Manchester Evening Mail*

The *Manchester Evening Chronicle*.

Index